The Morning Meeting Book

Roxann Kriete

with contributions by

Lynn Bechtel

STRATEGIES FOR TEACHERS SERIES

All net proceeds from the sale of *The Morning Meeting Book* support the work of Northeast Foundation for Children, Inc., a nonprofit educational organization whose mission is to foster safe, challenging, and joyful elementary classrooms and schools.

The stories in this book are all based on real events in the classroom. However, in order to respect the privacy of students, names and many identifying characteristics of students and situations have been changed.

ISBN: 978-1-892989-09-3

Library of Congress Control Number: 2002101348

Second edition April 2002

Photographs: Peter Wrenn, William Elwell, Cherry Wyman, Marlynn K. Clayton

Cover and book design: Woodward Design

NORTHEAST FOUNDATION FOR CHILDREN, INC.

85 Avenue A, Suite 204

P. O. Box 718

Turners Falls, MA 01376-0718

800-360-6332

www.responsiveclassroom.org

13   12   11   10   13   12   11   10

Printed on recycled paper

We would like to thank the Shinnyo-en Foundation for its generous support of the development of this book.

The mission of the Shinnyo-en Foundation is "to bring forth deeper compassion among humankind, to promote greater harmony, and to nurture future generations toward building more caring communities."

ACKNOWLEDGMENTS

Many people have contributed to the ideas and the articulation of those ideas in both the first edition and the expanded edition of this book.

The founders of Northeast Foundation for Children, who talked with me, critiqued my work, and offered permission to use materials they had created. Most significantly, they trusted me to articulate practices at the core of their life's work. Specifically, I want to acknowledge:

Jay Lord, for his conviction that I could and should write this and for shouldering additional work himself to clear my way.

Ruth Charney, for rich and provocative conversations, shared stories, support, and suggestions.

Marlynn Clayton, for taking the manuscript to the beach and for tending so carefully to its detail.

Chip Wood, for many introductions to teachers and schools and for bringing both his educator's and poet's sensibilities to his reading of this manuscript.

While preparing to write this book I visited schools in many towns and cities, and I drew from my experiences at Greenfield Center School, for many years the laboratory school for NEFC. I was inspired over and over by wise and powerful teachers—by their passion for learning and their devotion to the children in their care. I am grateful to the many teachers and students who welcomed me warmly into their classrooms to observe and to participate.

For their help in creating the expanded edition of *The Morning Meeting Book,* I'd like to thank:

Lynn Bechtel, for writing the chapter on Morning Meeting in middle schools, gathering additional greetings and activities, and serving as project manager for the expanded edition. Her thoughtful contributions have made the book richer and fuller and more useful to teachers of adolescents.

Kathy Brady, Ruth Charney, Linda Crawford, Anna Foot, Barbara Forshag, Jay Lord, and *Chip Wood,* for each of their unique roles in helping to shape Northeast Foundation for Children's work in middle schools and for their valuable contributions to the middle school chapter.

Bonnie Baer-Simahk, for generously sharing her knowledge of using Morning Meeting with second language learners.

Middle school teachers *Theresa Gammel* and *Lourdes Mercado* and the students in their seventh and eighth grade advisories at B. F. Brown Middle School, Fitchburg, Massachusetts, for welcoming us into their Morning Meetings and for their thoughtful comments about the value of Morning Meeting for middle school students.

Marlynn Clayton, for her ideas, suggestions, resources, and feedback that helped us update the appendices.

Alice Yang, for her precision and efficiency in copyediting and proofreading the new material.

Jeff and Leslie Woodward, designers, for the care they take with presentation and with people and, Jeff, for his painstaking proofreading of the first edition.

The support and companionship of many people was essential to the first edition. I remain grateful to:

Mary Beth Forton, project manager of the first edition and cherished office mate, for her special blend of keen intelligence and gentle care.

Marian Lubinsky, for countless cups of tea, teaching advice, stories, and laughter during the Friday afternoons of my first year of teaching. She taught me much of what I know about the value of collegial conversation.

Sharon Dunn, for the wide-ranging intelligence, wise counsel, and generosity of spirit which have infused her work as a long-time Board member and friend of NEFC.

Bob Strachota, for his willingness to examine his own teaching practice, for asking real questions, and for inviting me into the life of his classroom.

Allen Woods, for his editing of the first edition, done with precision and care.

Jean Truckey, for handling so much so capably during the preparation of the first edition.

Laurie Harrison, for her enthusiasm for the adventures of learning.

Joan Cenedella, for invigorating lunch conversations and for dropping in just when we needed her—and agreeing to stay a while.

Pam Porter, for her words of encouragement.

And always I am thankful for:

Eleanor and *Elsie,* mothers, whose example reminds me what love, hard work, and courage can achieve.

Russ and our children, Ben and Rachel, cherished family, for their love and support.

*To Sharon Dunn, long-time Northeast Foundation for Children
Board of Directors member, with gratitude for her love of words and learning,
her ability to blend dreaming and doing, and her belief in
and guidance of our publishing endeavors.*

TABLE OF CONTENTS

Just as we know instinctively that it makes sense to identify the most effective practices to teach a subject such as mathematics, take those practices and structure them into a sequenced curriculum, and implement that curriculum with trained professionals during dedicated classroom time, we must recognize now that the same effort must be mustered if we are to succeed in the social and emotional domains. It simply makes sense that if we are to expect children to be knowledgeable, responsible, and caring—and to be so despite significant obstacles—we must teach social and emotional skills, attitudes, and values with the same structure and attention that we devote to traditional subjects.

Maurice Elias et al.
Promoting Social and Emotional Learning:
Guidelines for Educators

"It Mattered that I Came"

In the spring of my first year as a secondary school teacher, I got a letter from a student for whom I had a particular fondness, letting me know that she was dropping out of school. School wasn't making much sense to her and little that she was being asked to learn held much interest for her. She wrote, almost apologetically, that school just wasn't a place she felt she belonged. More than twenty years later, her words still seem profoundly sad to me:

I will always remember how you said "Hi, Sue" as I walked into eighth period. It made me feel like it really mattered that I came.

It touched and pained me that something which seemed so small to me, an act I hadn't even been aware of, had meant so much to her. I vowed to learn something from it and became more intentional about greeting my students. I stationed myself by the door and tried to say a little something to each one as they entered, or at least to make eye contact and smile at every student, not just the ones like Sue for whom I had an instinctive affinity.

Gradually I realized how much I was learning at my post by the door. I observed who bounced in with head up and smile wide, whose eyes were red-rimmed from tears shed in the girls' room at lunch, who mumbled a response

Introduction

All classroom members—grown-ups and students—
gather in a circle at the start of every day for Morning Meeting.

into his collar and averted his eyes every day for an entire semester. I didn't know what to do about much of it, but at least I was learning how to notice.

I have learned a lot since then. It is good for students to be noticed, to be seen by their teacher. But it is only a start, not enough by itself. They must notice and be noticed by each other as well.

Years after I taught Sue, I joined the staff of Greenfield Center School, the independent K–8 school founded by Northeast Foundation for Children. There, I saw teachers teaching students to greet each other, to speak to each other, to listen to each other. I saw students start each day together in Morning Meeting where noticing and being noticed were explicit goals. This book is about Morning Meeting—a particular and deliberate way to begin the school day. Today, many children in kindergartens, elementary, and middle schools around the country launch their school days in Morning Meetings.

All classroom members—grown-ups and students—gather in a circle, greet each other, and listen and respond to each others' news. We take note of who is present and who is absent; whether it is still raining or not; who is smiling and buoyant; who is having a hard time smiling. We briefly grapple with problems that challenge our minds and look forward to the events in the day ahead. Morning Meeting allows us to begin each day as a community of caring and respectful learners.

Morning Meeting Format

Morning Meeting is made up of four, sequential components and lasts up to a total of a half hour each day. Although there is much overlap, each component has its own purposes and structure. The components intentionally provide opportunities for children to practice the skills of greeting, listening and responding, group problem solving, and noticing and anticipating. The daily practice of these four components gradually weaves a web that binds a class together.

1. Greeting: Children greet each other by name, often including handshaking, clapping, singing, and other activities.

2. Sharing: Students share some news of interest to the class and respond to each other, articulating their thoughts, feelings, and ideas in a positive manner.

3. Group Activity: The whole class does a short activity together, building class cohesion through active participation.

4. Morning Message: Students practice academic skills and warm up for the day ahead by reading and discussing a daily message posted for them.

Teachers must commit more than just time to implement Morning Meeting. They must also commit themselves to a belief in children's capacity to take care of themselves and each other as they learn social skills like respect and responsibility along with academic skills like vocabulary and algorithms. Morning Meeting creates opportunities for children to practice these social skills. It also creates opportunities for teachers to model these skills and give children valuable feedback. It provides practice in respectful behavior and helps children stretch the boundaries of their social world.

The time one commits to Morning Meeting is an investment which is repaid many times over. The sense of belonging and the skills of attention, listening, expression, and cooperative interaction developed in Morning Meeting are a foundation for every lesson, every transition time, every lining-up, every upset and conflict, all day and all year long. Morning Meeting is a microcosm of the way we wish our schools to be—communities full of learning, safe and respectful and challenging for all.

The
*Responsive
Classroom*
Approach

How to
Use This
Book

The *Responsive Classroom*® Approach

The Morning Meeting format described in this book was developed by Northeast Foundation for Children staff as part of the *Responsive Classroom* approach to teaching and learning. It is an approach informed by belief in seven basic tenets.

The Responsive Classroom

1. **The social curriculum is as important as the academic curriculum.**

2. **How children learn is as important as what children learn.**

3. **The greatest cognitive growth occurs through social interaction.**

4. **There is a set of social skills that children need to learn and practice in order to be successful. They form the acronym CARES—cooperation, assertion, responsibility, empathy, self-control.**

5. **We must know our children individually, culturally, and developmentally.**

6. **Knowing the families of the children we teach is as important as knowing the children.**

7. **Teachers and administrators must model the social and academic skills that they wish to teach their students.**

How to Use This Book

You may choose to read the entire book from beginning to end, select sections which immediately grab your attention, or use it as a reference as your Morning Meeting experience grows. The book begins with a fundamental chapter about Morning Meeting as a whole, followed by chapters about each of its four components, a chapter about Morning Meeting in middle schools, and a conclusion. The structure is designed to tell three things about Morning Meeting: what it is, why it is, and how to do it.

In the classroom

Each component chapter begins with a section that shows Morning Meeting in action. Some of these vignettes are from large, urban schools; some are from small, rural schools. Though the demographics vary widely, the spirit and elements of the Morning Meetings are consistent, the children and their teachers familiar to those of us who spend time in schools. These glimpses take you into the middle of classrooms where Morning Meetings are flourishing.

Purposes and reflections

These articulate the purposes and goals of each component and locate connections to theory and the larger context of learning. They are like a guided tour, highlighting and interpreting some of the powerful moments created in our classrooms and conveying some of the specific details and flavor of well-run Morning Meetings.

Getting started

These sections offer directions for teachers as they begin to implement the components of Morning Meeting. Directions and examples of teacher language are offered as templates to be used for guidance, not as exact patterns for repetition. Your knowledge of your class's development, pace, needs, and of your own teaching style will lead to adaptations that work best for you and your class.

These directions are offered with respect for individual teachers and a wish to empower them. They are offered, also, with the awareness, affirmed by thousands of teachers with whom we have worked, that templates drawn by experienced hands are invaluable tools when starting something new. Feel free to use these templates—trace them, adapt them, refine them—so that they truly serve you. Just keep the purposes and goals of Morning Meeting in mind.

Each *Getting Started* section ends with a concise listing of teacher and student responsibilities to help you implement Morning Meeting and assess your practice.

Fine tunings

These questions and answers address some concerns and issues teachers commonly encounter as their experience with Morning Meeting evolves. This section considers some of the questions teachers frequently ask as they move past the basic introduction of Morning Meeting in their classrooms. These particular questions have surfaced frequently in our own practice and in teaching other teachers over the years.

Morning Meeting

AN OVERVIEW

It's time, it's time, it's time for Morning Meeting now..." The melody, begun by the teacher and picked up by the students, drifts down the hall from the kindergarten classroom. Directly upstairs, in a fourth grade room, a student selects the wooden chime from its resting place on a shelf top and strikes it gently with a mallet. When her classmates quiet down and look at her, she announces simply, "Morning Meeting time." Next door, the teacher of the fifth and sixth graders puts his coffee mug on a counter and rings the old-fashioned school bell which is the signal in his room to stop and listen. "Five minute warning. Finish your plans for the day and come to the rug for Morning Meeting."

Teachers and students crave a certain amount of predictability and routine in the school day, especially at the start. The format of Morning Meeting is predictable, but there is plenty of room for variation and change. Meetings reflect the style and flavor of individual teachers and groups. They also reflect the ebb and flow of a school year's seasons—September's new shoes and anxious, careful faces; December's pre-holiday excitement; February's endless runny noses; April's spring-has-sprung exuberance. Its mixture of routine and surprise, of comfort and challenge, make Morning Meeting a treasured and flexible teaching tool.

PURPOSES AND REFLECTIONS

**Purposes
and
Reflections**

The socialization of children has historically been considered an important part of preschools and kindergartens. Learning to play together, to listen to each other, to wait in line are skills that have long been a legitimate part of the early childhood curriculum. But Lilian Katz, noted early childhood educator, sees significant benefits for structured interactions beyond the earliest grades: "There is quite a bit to learn from early childhood education experiences that can be 'pushed up' to later grades, instead of the classic pushing down." (Katz 1998, 8)

Preschool and early childhood programs traditionally begin with a ritual, often called Circle Time. During Circle Time, children gather for a song, practice counting, take attendance, and share. Morning Meeting evolved from this accepted practice, building on children's needs for social guidance, structure, and interaction. Morning Meeting is a translation of Circle Time for older students, "pushing up" the goals of socialization and using our detailed knowledge of students' social, emotional, and cognitive development.

Educators have learned that social skills are not a checklist to be mastered by the end of kindergarten so that students can get on with the acquisition of academic skills. Instead, social skills are skills we continue to acquire and refine throughout our lives, just like academic skills.

At every age, children need opportunities to practice and define these skills as part of a group. At five, it may be hard to share the box of crayons; at eleven, it is hard to share a friend. At seven, it is a matter of pride to clean the lunchroom table neatly; at thirteen, it is a matter of pride to disdain the same chore. As Dr. Arnold Gesell concluded from his extensive research on child development, growth is not a straight line function. (Ilg et al. 1981) It loops and spirals and zigs and zags, its pattern influenced by characteristics of each person's age, background, and individual temperament.

Teachers have long known and researchers are now confirming that social skills are not just something to be taught so that children behave well enough to get on with the real business of schooling. Rather, they are inextricably intertwined with cognitive growth and intellectual progress. A person who can listen well, who can frame a good question and has the assertiveness to pose it, who can examine a situation from a number of perspectives will be a strong learner. All those skills—skills essential to academic achievement—must be modeled, experienced, practiced, extended, and refined in the context of social interaction. Morning Meeting is a forum in which all that happens. It is not an add-on, something extra to make time for, but rather an integral part of the day's planning and curriculum.

Morning Meeting makes important contributions to the tone and content of a classroom. The following broad statements summarize these contributions and each is explored in a section that follows.

Purposes of Morning Meeting

1. **Morning Meeting sets the tone for respectful learning and establishes a climate of trust.**

2. **The tone and climate of Morning Meeting extend beyond the Meeting.**

3. **Morning Meeting motivates children by addressing two human needs: the need to feel a sense of significance and belonging and the need to have fun.**

4. **The repetition of many ordinary moments of respectful interaction in Morning Meeting enables some extraordinary moments.**

5. **Morning Meeting merges social, emotional, and intellectual learning.**

Morning Meeting sets the tone for respectful learning and establishes a climate of trust.

Beginnings can be critical. The leader of a workshop I recently attended asked our group of teachers and principals to recall and describe our first half hour as teachers. A good number of participants were nearing retirement age and their first moments as teachers were more than thirty years ago, but every one of us could recall in vivid detail what happened and how we felt in those first thirty minutes.

Certainly, the first thirty minutes of each day are not as momentous or embedded in memory as the first thirty minutes in a new career. There are some days, in fact, when we can hardly remember at four o'clock in the afternoon what happened at nine o'clock that morning. The details may have flown from our cluttered memory, but it is likely that the pace and flavor of our first half

*Morning Meeting helps to create a climate of trust
that encourages children to take risks.*

**Purposes
of Morning
Meeting**

hour in school had a lot to do with the way we felt at four o'clock and whether the day's challenges felt exhilarating or overwhelming. The same is true for our students. Beginnings matter.

The way we begin each day in our classroom sets the tone for learning and speaks volumes about what and whom we value, about our expectations for the way we will treat each other, and about the way we believe learning occurs.

Children's learning begins the second they walk in the doors of the building. Children notice whether they are greeted warmly or overlooked, whether the classroom feels chaotic and unpredictable, or ordered and comforting. If they announce, "My cat got hit by a car last night but it's gonna' be all right," they may find an interested, supportive audience or one that turns away. Every detail of their experience informs students about their classroom and their place in it.

When we start the day with everyone together, face-to-face, welcoming each person, sharing news, listening to individual voices, and communicating as a caring group, we make several powerful statements. We say that every person matters. We say that the way we interact individually and as a group matters. We say that our culture is one of friendliness and thoughtfulness. We say that hard work can be accomplished and important discoveries can be made by playing together. We say that teachers hold authority, even though they are a part of the circle. We say that this is a place where courtesy and warmth and safety reign—a place of respect for all.

In order to learn, we must take risks—offering up a tentative answer we are far from sure is right or trying out a new part in the choir when we are not sure we can hit the notes. We can take these risks only when we know we will be respected and valued, no matter the outcome. We must trust in order to risk, and Morning Meeting helps create a climate of trust.

The tone and climate of Morning Meeting extend beyond the Meeting.

We see this in any number of ways. For instance, children may begin to greet each other spontaneously, even before the Meeting circle has convened. A first grade teacher whose class had been using Morning Meeting for several months wrote: "One Tuesday as I stood by the door, waiting for the class to gather, I just watched. They were genuinely glad to see each other. Some were hugging a greeting. Some were clapping for something. What a joy to watch—I was merely an observer and just loved it."

Sometimes what transfers isn't a specific behavior, such as a greeting, but is instead an attitude. Ruth Charney, author and teacher at the Greenfield Center School, described this scene from the seventh/eighth grade room she co-taught.

"Time for Meeting," announced the teacher and the students assembled on the low benches arranged around the perimeter of their whole group meeting area. Three students hung back, whispering by the coat rack.

Their teacher addressed them pleasantly: "Daria, Abby, Lindsay, Meeting is starting." The girls exchanged looks and moved toward the circle, pointedly ignoring the space others had made for them, sitting instead on the floor a few feet behind one of the benches. Clearly, they had come into the room with their own agenda.

Their teacher, voice still pleasant but firm, looked straight at them: "You need to move into the circle." They hesitated a moment but then moved as directed.

Quietly, using the structure of the circle, their teacher reminded them of an expecta-tion: You will be fully part of this classroom, not outside of it. Within a few minutes, the three back-benchers were absorbed by a classmate's announcement that a moose had wandered through his backyard that morning.

When Meeting was over, off they went to math groups, chatting with others along the way, their agenda defused, able to be positive participants in classroom life that day.

Morning Meeting motivates children by addressing two human needs: the need to feel a sense of significance and belonging, and the need to have fun.

All of us need to feel that we belong and are valued for the competencies, skills, and knowledge we bring to a group, that our unique contributions are recognized and appreciated. All the components of Morning Meeting speak to those needs directly.

Consulting teacher Melissa Correa-Connolly of Leominster, Massachusetts, speaks of what she has seen happen, both in her own elementary classroom and in the rooms of many teachers with whom she has worked:

"I think of Morning Meeting as having such immense power because it meets the emotional needs of children. It acknowledges everyone and makes them feel significant. It does away with the feeling many children have of being a piece of furniture in the classroom. Morning Meeting is the first thing in the morning and it allows children to be seen, to have a voice."

Having fun is also a universal human need. Fun is not necessarily synonymous with frivolity or silliness, though it can sometimes be both. It does mean engagement and fascination with what we do. Fun is playful and light-hearted even when the activity is hard and the challenge great. It is not about winning, but about immersion in the pleasure of the activity itself.

Fun might involve striving to find the five punctuation errors planted in the morning message or learning to sing "Dona Nobis Pacem" in three-part

Purposes of Morning Meeting

Morning Meeting is full of opportunities to have fun together.

harmony. It might mean trying to guess the three-digit number a classmate is thinking of in a game called "Pico, Fermé, Nada" *(Appendix F).* Fun might mean laughing when serious and dignified Amy reports on her new puppy's antics, or it might mean learning a new and lively greeting EJ brought back from summer camp.

Fun is also connected with risk-taking. Risks taken in a playful way can teach us how to handle the more serious risks that growth can demand. The children (and adults) who don't play often have a difficult time reaching their potential because growth almost always requires venturing into the unknown.

One thing is certain. Humans strive to fulfill their needs in whatever way they can, whether those ways are positive or negative. The child who can't be known or recognized in the group for friendly contributions will be known for his trouble-making contributions. And when our programs don't provide constructive ways to meet our students' needs for fun, the students will devise their own, often not-so-constructive ways.

Overview

Morning Meeting is full of opportunities for a class to have fun together and for all its members to feel a sense of significance and belonging, needs affirmed by theory and research: "Adler (1930) proposed that a sense of belonging motivates children to develop their skills and contribute to the welfare of all.... Research indicates that educators who establish firm boundaries, foster warm personal relationships in the classroom, and enable students to have an impact on their environment strengthen students' attachment to their school, their interest in learning, their ability to refrain from self-destructive behaviors, and their positive behaviors." (Elias et al. 1997, 44)

The repetition of many ordinary moments of respectful interaction in Morning Meeting enables some extraordinary moments.

Morning Meeting, repeated every day, is full of moments that by themselves seem quite mundane and ordinary. But this repetition can enable some quite extraordinary accomplishments within and beyond the Meeting circle, too. Consider this story told by a third grade teacher from a school where Morning Meetings were an established part of school life in all the classrooms:

One wintry Tuesday morning at about 9:30, just as Morning Meeting in my room was ending, a second grader from the classroom adjacent to mine entered and approached me politely. "Excuse me, Mrs. Truesdell, but our teacher isn't here yet. We finished Morning Meeting, but we don't know what to do next."

A series of missed communications including a school secretary with the flu and a faulty answering machine had resulted in a class without a teacher or a substitute. These seven-year-olds knew the routines so well that they had gathered themselves and conducted an orderly and merry Morning Meeting. I remembered, in fact, hearing the strains of the song "River" wafting through the thin wall that connected the two rooms and thinking how much better it sounded than last week!

These children's daily participation in the ongoing routines of Morning Meeting had enabled them to take responsibility for these routines even in the absence of their teacher. Their school celebrated their responsible behavior at an assembly later that week.

The habits of participation established by Morning Meeting routines can also serve a community well in more extreme circumstances. The experience of Joyce Love, a revered elementary school teacher in Washington, DC, testifies to this.

Purposes of Morning Meeting

As a part of Morning Meeting, her class knew how to come quickly together and how to listen respectfully to each other. They had considered hard questions such as "What can you say when someone shares something that's really upsetting to them?" as well as "What might we say when someone shares something that makes them really happy?" They had, under Joyce's guidance, carefully constructed habits of participation and practiced them day-in and day-out in the most ordinary situations with the most ordinary material—news of a swimming test passed, a baby brother with chicken pox, a visit from relatives.

One morning, several of Joyce's students saw a dead body on a street corner on their walk to school. Now, when they were confronted with an event of monumental impact, they had a familiar circle to come to. They had patterns of sharing and response that helped their teacher to help them begin to deal with a haunting scene. "If it hadn't been for Morning Meeting, I wouldn't have known what to do. Its structures helped take care of things," recalled Joyce.

Not all extraordinary moments enabled by Morning Meeting are tragic, of course. At Greenfield Center School, eighth graders take a literature course that calls upon them to consider the universal themes of the literary tradition, what educator and author Parker Palmer calls the "big stories" (Palmer 1998), and relate them to the "little stories" of students' own lives, the stories that tell their personal and individual tales.

For the final assignment, each student writes a play based on an event important in his or her life. Students cast and direct these plays, with fellow class members as actors, and present them at Play Night for their families, faculty, and friends. Some plays are light, some somber. One might be elaborately plotted with a dozen characters and several settings; the next might be a minimalist dialogue.

All are presentations by a group of young teens relying on each other to make, in Palmer's language, these "little" stories "big," to make art from what they have witnessed in their lives. It is a profound exercise and everyone does it, not just one gifted group, year after year.

Inspired by attending many years of Play Nights, a Center School parent who taught at a local high school tried the same assignment with her literature class. Despite a year with them in which they studied hard and well together, she reported that it failed. An essential ingredient was missing, she realized. That ingredient was trust.

They knew how to write dialogue and paint sets. But sharing things of import to them and trusting in a respectful response—that was another level entirely. In the end, the plays were superficial and the students' commitment to them half-hearted.

Are the Center School plays the product of one year of literature study? Only in part. True, they emerge with the help of an inspiring teacher, at a transitional moment when students are keenly aware of their impending graduation and are poised to look back as they step ahead. But it is also true that they are the product of a group of students who have practiced the Morning Meeting skills of communication and community every day of their school lives for as much as nine years.

They have used their voices to greet, sing, laugh, console, and celebrate within their Meeting circles for all those mornings of all those years. And on Play Night, those voices join an ensemble and speak, not just to each other across the circle, but to the larger audience which they face from the stage. They are oh-so-ready. And Morning Meeting helped get them there.

Morning Meeting merges social, emotional, and intellectual learning.

Morning Meeting provides an arena where distinctions that define social, emotional, and academic skills fade, and learning becomes an integrated experience. Parker Palmer describes his vision of an educational community as one that depends on a dynamic dialogue about things that matter. He states, "Truth is an eternal conversation about things that matter, conducted with passion and discipline.... But it is not our knowledge of conclusions that keeps us in the truth. It is our commitment to the conversation itself, our willingness to put forward our observations and interpretations for testing by the community and to return the favor to others. To be in the truth, we must know how to observe and reflect and speak and listen, with passion and with discipline, in the circle gathered around a given subject." (Palmer 1998, 104)

In Morning Meeting, the circle "gathers around" many subjects, some introduced by the teacher, some by the children. In the dialogue of the circle, we stretch each others' understandings, using the skills which Palmer names: observing, reflecting, speaking, listening.

A consulting teacher tells of a Morning Meeting she led in a classroom she visited in a distant city. The newspaper headline that morning told of a citywide water contamination crisis. At Morning Meeting, she shared that she had seen that headline and asked these third graders what they knew about the water problem in their city.

Her question triggered an outpouring of knowledge. They knew, in fact, a great deal. She listened and noted the facts on a chart. As the listing of what they knew reached an end, the talk turned to what they didn't know but wondered about. Those questions, too, were noted on the chart, along with some hypotheses. Another teacher from the school observed the Meeting and was incredulous. "Those kids must have been rehearsed; they couldn't know that much!"

This conversation, within the structured safety of Morning Meeting, allowed learners to put forward what conclusions they knew, to pose questions and venture possible interpretations. They were able to "observe and reflect and speak and listen" communally about a subject that mattered very much to them.

In the wonderful book *On Their Way,* listening and talking are deemed "the power tools." (Fraser and Skolnick 1994, 145) Recognizing this, many school systems now endorse cooperative learning activities and approaches in classrooms, and there is much talk about the skills of collaboration needed to move into the next decades. Morning Meeting sharpens the tools of listening and talking which are essential for partner chats, small group discussions, peer critiquing, and other cooperative learning strategies.

See *Appendix A* for a full listing of the myriad social, emotional, and intellectual skills children are learning as they gather together in Morning Meeting.

Purposes of Morning Meeting

GETTING STARTED

Establish a set schedule for Morning Meeting.

Ideally, Morning Meeting happens every day. The best time is first thing in the morning after most children have arrived and settled in. Schedule twenty to thirty minutes for Morning Meeting, depending upon the age of the children in your class. You may wish to reconsider your schedule as the year progresses. The class that squirmed their way raggedly through ten minutes of meeting time in September may be quite ready for double that time by November.

It is important, even with older students, to keep Morning Meetings from going on too long. It is also important to plan for a change of pace immediately following Morning Meeting. When it is followed by an academic period requiring continued sitting in a circle, it can be deadly for even the most focused and attentive students. Even a few minutes of an activity which requires some moving around provides the needed variation.

Overview

Many teachers of young children have found that a separate "Sharing" meeting at a predictable time later in the day is more productive. The attention and focus that students can give each other during Sharing is more important than the time of day that it happens.

Morning Meeting sharpens children's
speaking and listening skills.

Introduce Morning Meeting to your students.

Explain to students that you will begin each day with a meeting—Morning
Meeting. Share with them your hopes and goals for this part of the day. Your
list might sound something like this:

- I hope that we will all get to know one another—not just our best friends.

- I want us to be able to practice taking care of each other so that we can all
  feel good about being in this class.

- I want us to be able to share different experiences and ideas.

- I want us to have fun together.

If your students are already familiar with Morning Meeting from previous
years, ask them to share their hopes and goals for this part of the day.

Getting Started

Communicate with parents about Morning Meeting.

Parents are very supportive of Morning Meeting when they understand its format and goals. If their first impression is formed from a child's report of a "new
game we played at Morning Meeting," they may draw the mistaken conclusion
that this is time taken away from learning. A letter to parents giving them a
glimpse of this part of their child's day and describing the learning integral to it,
can give them a framework in which to place the accounts they hear from their
children. Good communication will help parents see Morning Meeting for the
vital learning time that it is.

A sample letter is included in *Appendix B*. Feel free to use it as a template,
adapting it to your school and your class. You might also consider talking about
Morning Meeting at a Parent Night, or PTA meeting, maybe even structuring
a piece of the parents' meeting in Morning Meeting format. Encourage parents
to visit the classroom and join in a Morning Meeting.

Phase in the implementation of Morning Meeting.

Acquaint your class with one component of Morning Meeting at a time, introducing and modeling each. (See the *Getting Started* section for each component
in the following chapters.) When you sense that students are comfortable and
ready for more, then add a component. Though this isn't their eventual order,
the most successful order of introduction is: Greeting, Group Activity, Morning
Message, and Sharing.

A plan for the first day might involve teaching children how to get into a circle, and then singing a song. On the second day, a greeting might be taught after the circle has formed. A few days later, the Morning Message chart might be introduced with a message as simple as "Welcome." Full Morning Meeting might not happen for several weeks.

Factors like the age and school experience of your students will influence your decision about timing. Your knowledge of your class will determine how quickly you add components. A carefully paced and deliberate introduction of new components, with time to practice and reflect, will pay off in the end.

Choose and teach signals you will use consistently.

It is essential to have simple, effective signals to get students' attention. Raising your voice is often neither simple nor effective, and if students are still involved in conversation or activity, chances are that many will not absorb the announcement.

Overview

Instead, teachers have found various non-verbal signals that say to students: "Stop what you are doing and give me (or a student who may be about to make an announcement) your attention." Some teachers ring a chime, bell, or triangle; others turn the classroom lights off, then on. When you have the attention

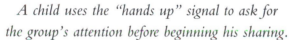

A child uses the "hands up" signal to ask for the group's attention before beginning his sharing.

of all students, make a brief statement. "Five minutes till Morning Meeting. Put away what you are working on and come to the Meeting area."

A "hands up" signal is useful to bring quiet and attention once the Meeting circle is formed. These signals are not exclusively for teacher use, but are available for responsible use by students as well. The same respect and response is expected whether a signal originates with a student or teacher, as in the following example.

It is Jonas's turn to share. He brought his gerbil, Harry, who has been waiting in his cage on a table in the corner. When Jonas leaves the circle to get Harry, many conversations commence. Jonas comes back, ready to share, but his classmates continue to chatter. He raises his hand. Across the circle, Amanda notices and raises hers. She gently elbows Leisha, next to her, who is whispering to Damien. Up goes Leisha's hand and she stops in mid-sentence and looks at Jonas. Around the circle hands go up and silence spreads. It is simple and efficient, with not a word of scolding or blame issued. His audience is ready and Jonas begins. "This is Harry. He's really a she..."

Getting Started

**The logistics of Morning Meeting are important.
Consider and teach them carefully.**

Over and over in our teaching lives, we are reminded not to make assumptions about what children know. Details about forming the circle for Morning Meeting and about coming to the circle with hands empty demand careful instruction at the outset and vigilant monitoring even when routines are established.

Understanding the "why" behind the details helps. Discuss why the circle is important to Morning Meeting. Talk about why it's important not to be clicking pens and rustling papers during Morning Meeting.

These discussions vary with the ages and readiness of students. I have heard six-year-olds offer simple and profound explanations: "A circle makes it possible for every person to see every other person. It has no front or back." I have heard twelve-year-olds engage in thoughtful and sophisticated discussions about different classroom arrangements—desks in rows, lecture halls, round seminar tables—and what sort of activity each promotes.

Many classes sit on the floor for Morning Meeting. Other classes seem to handle themselves better, or feel recognized as older, when seated in chairs. There is no single correct way. What's important is that the circle creates an open and inviting space which allows for a group activity and encourages a comfortable but attentive attitude.

If students need to move furniture to clear a space large enough for the whole class to make a circle, or if they need to move their chairs over to the circle area, talk about how it can be done smoothly.

"We will need to move our chairs in a way that takes care of our room and the people in it. What are some things we will need to think about so that we can do it safely and efficiently?" poses the teacher to her third grade class.

"Not scuffing the floors."

"Be careful not to hit anybody with your chair by accident."

"Put chairs down softly so we don't bother the kindergartners on the first floor."

A bit of modeling helps. *"Show me, Shannon, how you can get your chair into the circle in a way that does all those things we just talked about. What do you think, class?"* Practice it. Reflect about how it went. *"Let's time ourselves. Was it safe? Was it efficient? On a scale of one to five, rate how we managed it."* (For more about how to use modeling as a teaching strategy, see *Appendix C.)*

Overview

Meeting rules vary depending on the age and needs of a group.
The rules on the left were generated by a group of first graders,
and the rules on the right were created by a group of
fifth and sixth graders.

Generate Morning Meeting rules with the students.

After students are comfortable with a couple of the components of Morning Meeting, refer to the goals named and pose a question which will establish a basic set of meeting procedures. "How can we take care of ourselves and each other so that our hopes for Morning Meeting can happen? What will we need to do?"

Implicit in the stance of this question is a view of rules as a social necessity generated by the community involved, not an arbitrary and disconnected list of imperatives. Answers will likely include some variation of the following:

- Listen

- Look at the person who's talking

Getting Started
- Keep your body in control

- Raise your hand if you want to talk

- Keep your hands down when someone is speaking

- Don't laugh at anyone

For many of the rules, a definition of terms is in order. Children are much more able to follow rules when they are defined in concrete terms.

"Listen!" volunteers a kindergartner.

"And how will someone who's speaking know that you're listening?" asks his teacher. A discussion of some of the finer points of listening etiquette follows: your eyes are on the person; you try not to wiggle; if you have to go to the bathroom, you try to wait until the person is done talking. Indeed, those are hallmarks of quality listening for five- and six-year-olds.

"Be respectful," offers a ten-year-old earnestly. "For sure," endorses her teacher. "And how do people show respect in a meeting?"

When a simple list and a common understanding of the rules have been reached, a poster with these rules displayed near the Meeting area can be a helpful reminder.

Give students responsibility in Morning Meeting.

Virtually every moment in Morning Meeting is laden with opportunities for students to assume responsibility in the community we call our classroom. They are responsible for making someone feel welcome, asking a thoughtful question,

Meetings are rich with opportunities for students to assume responsibility and actively participate.

making a kind comment, solving a "puzzler" question on the chart. In some classrooms, once Morning Meeting is familiar and established, students also take turns leading the whole Meeting or selected parts of it.

We must give our students real responsibility in Morning Meeting; we must believe that they can be trusted and will be successful in meeting the expectations we hold. This can be difficult, particularly for those of us who gained much of our experience in more teacher-centered settings. We may be accustomed to being the dispensers of information and the handers-out of papers. It can be a tricky business to step back from the center, while remaining in control.

Pay attention to your role as teacher.

Make no mistake: Successful Morning Meetings require a teacher who is in control in the classroom. As teachers we are interpreters, synthesizers, balance-keepers, time-keepers, and safety-net holders. Even when students are leading a section of Meeting, we are watchful and often intervene with a reframing question, a quick suggestion, or redirection.

What is required of us in this role may be simple and straightforward. "Choose one more person for a question or comment, Danita," we say when many hands are raised and time is running short; "Join the circle, Todd," to a boy who always wants to hang back.

Other times, discerning and guiding the dynamics in Morning Meeting can be more complex. Jeremy continually shares complicated details of "scary science" stories about mutant viruses, colliding asteroids, and toxic pesticides which invisibly saturate strawberries. He is a highly knowledgeable child and his graphic details are accurate and documented.

His teacher wonders about the effect of this stream of threatening news, so authoritatively presented, upon his eleven-year-old peers. Are they terrified, challenged, or humiliated by their relative lack of factual knowledge? Is this a positive way for Jeremy to define a niche in the class? Careful observation and perhaps a one-on-one chat with Jeremy outside of Meeting will inform his teacher as she contemplates whether her intervention is needed to protect either Jeremy or the class.

Getting Started

Bob Strachota, author and teacher at the Greenfield Center School, tells a story of a child he coached in soccer who commented, "I like how you taught us soccer. You were always in the middle, but never in the way." The teacher's role in Morning Meeting is a bit like that. We are not the center, but we are central.

Pay attention to the management aspects of Morning Meeting and hold children to the expectations you have named together.

Addressing what can seem like small details—whom students greet, where they sit, which students are rarely the recipients of thoughtful comments—sends two messages: you value the skills and attitudes that specific actions reflect and you believe in the capacity of your students to accomplish them.

For Morning Meeting to flourish, we must let children know that we are as serious about their behavior and skills during this time as we are during reading group or math group. Let them know by your comments that you notice how they are doing with the named expectations, and that you will hold them to those expectations, helping them by reminders and directions when they need them. Frame your comments in the positive, focusing upon what students are doing right or upon helping them identify what would be a better way, rather than naming what it is they are not doing.

You may think of these sorts of comments as the "three R's"—reinforcing, reminding, or redirecting comments. Here are some examples:

Reinforcing

- I notice the way everyone remembered to smile at the person they greeted today.
- I notice lots of people sitting next to different classmates each day.
- Most people are remembering to read the message chart when they enter our room in the morning.
- I notice how quickly and quietly we moved our chairs into a circle this morning.

Reminding

- Before we move to the Meeting rug, remind me what you will think about as you choose where to sit.
- Who remembers what to do if you forget the name of someone you want to greet?
- Laurie, remind me, what do we need to remember as we move our chairs into the circle?

Redirecting

- I hear a lot of chair legs dragging across the floor. Show me, Jonah, how we can hold our chairs when we move them so that they don't scuff the floor.
- Today you must sit next to someone of the opposite gender, Cheryl.
- I see that a lot of people are looking at things that others brought for Sharing. Show me where we could put these things so that we can give our attention to the person speaking.

Morning Meeting responsibilities

In implementing and assessing Morning Meeting, keep the following general responsibilities in mind.

Teachers' responsibilities

- **To make sure the space is adequate and appropriate for the component. Can a circle form? Can all be seen? Can a particular game be safely played?**

- **To act as timekeeper, keeping things moving**

- **To facilitate the Meeting, making sure that all children are greeted, that a variety of children are responding to sharing, that the tone is respectful, etc.**

Getting Started

- **To observe students' skills—both social and academic**

- **To notice behaviors and to reinforce, remind, and redirect using positive language**

- **To make sure that there is equal opportunity to participate, that gender or personality traits aren't dictating participation patterns**

- **To make sure everyone in the classroom (paraprofessionals, visitors, parents, etc.) is included in the Meeting**

Students' responsibilities

- **To get to Meeting promptly and to form the circle safely and efficiently**

- **To participate fully—contributing actively, listening well, and responding appropriately**

- **To interact with a variety of classmates in the good spirit of Morning Meeting**

- **To move smoothly from Meeting to the next activity**

FINE TUNINGS

Q. *Most of my students really are great at Morning Meeting, but a couple of my students just can't sit still and behave themselves. How can I help them be part of Meeting and not disrupt it?*

A. Children vary a great deal in their ability to follow Meeting rules. The teacher's knowledge of the individual child is the starting point for any action. Is the child younger than most peers and simply not yet ready for the expectations that are appropriate for the rest of the group? Are there special needs that make participation particularly challenging?

For the child who is simply too young, a special arrangement about the length of time he attends Morning Meeting makes sense. Give a signal that will let him know when he is to leave the circle, and discuss what he'll do during the remaining Meeting time. Gradually, as he is successful with sitting still, extend the time he spends in Meeting.

Sometimes a bit of situational assistance is all that is needed. "Miranda, I notice that you have a hard time listening to other people when you sit next to Molly. You need to pick a different place to sit at Morning Meeting."

Or to the fidgeter whose fancy gizmo-watch treats everyone to a rendition of three electronic verses of "The Yellow Rose of Texas" at least twice in every Meeting, "Your watch needs to be in your cubby during Morning Meeting, Gerard."

Some children with lots of overflowing energy are better able to concentrate if they have something that quietly occupies their hands during Meeting. Is this fair, some may ask, when the rule is to come to Meeting empty-handed? This is a complex question about justice that repeats itself with variations all through our lives.

Fair treatment is responsive to individual needs and doesn't always mean treating people with a cookie-cutter sameness. When students trust that their needs, too, will be met in the same spirit of fairness, they are generally able to understand and accept these modifications.

Occasionally, a child's special needs require more elaborate intervention. I saw a skillful example of this a few years ago in a fourth/fifth grade inclusion classroom. Andrew was a fifth grader whose special needs manifested in blurting out inappropriate and rude remarks often unconnected to anything preceding them. Early in the first weeks of the school year, it was clear that he was not

Overview

ready to be part of group sharing, that he needed some very specialized and intensive instruction in order to participate in this part of Meeting.

So, every day, when it was time for Sharing, Andrew and one of his teachers, Ms. Scamardella (Ms. S.), left the circle and moved to a table in the opposite corner of the room where Andrew had "private sharing" with Ms. S. while co-teacher Ms. Daggett continued the Meeting. In his "private sharing," Andrew practiced sharing a piece of news appropriately, with no swearing or name-calling. Ms. S. modeled careful patterns of suitable responses. Then she shared a piece of news and helped him learn to choose a polite response and practice it.

After a few months, Andrew was able to rejoin the group for Sharing, listening quietly most days, and on a really good day, offering a comment or a question "on the spot." Andrew's own sharing to the group was scheduled for Friday each week, sharing which he planned and rehearsed a few minutes each day, Monday through Thursday, with Ms. S.

Fine Tunings

This example is more extreme than most, but it illustrates a couple of important principles. Just as different groups are ready for the phasing in of Morning Meeting components at different rates, individual children may be ready at different rates also. While children should participate in Morning Meeting as much as they can with as little modification as possible, if their participation is "stuck" in the negative, if they are spending more time in the time-out chair than in the Meeting circle, then clearly the teacher must pay special attention and address the situation.

Q. *I have several children who frequently come in late, and a couple who have to leave in the middle of Meeting for special programs. Should they be part of Meeting?*

A. Yes, definitely. Morning Meeting is for everyone. Latecomers should be greeted pleasantly and welcomed without unduly disrupting whatever is happening in Meeting. In order to minimize the disruption while still making the latecomer feel welcome, some teachers assign a child the daily job of welcoming latecomers into the circle.

Meeting time itself is not the time to address the tardiness, frustrating as it may be. If it is an occasional lateness, simply help the child fit into the flow of the day. If it is a chronic problem with a particular child, then some investigation is in order. Do they walk to school? Dawdle once they're in the building? Do parents drop them off on the way to work?

Sometimes a chat with the student alone is enough; other times parents' help is needed. And sometimes, no matter how many phone calls and discussions of the importance of beginning the day with the class and how promptness implicitly communicates respect and responsibility, there is little progress.

In the case of students who have to leave early for "specials," make sure that Greeting can happen with them in the circle and teach them how to leave the circle quietly and unobtrusively when it is time. If the same students must leave every day, you might think about scheduling a separate "Sharing" meeting near the end of the day when everyone can attend. And for younger children who are not yet able to read the chart independently, make sure they are aware of any announcements about the day included in the chart.

Q. *Children are really comfortable with our Morning Meeting, maybe too comfortable. Even I sometimes feel like it's boring. Help!*

A. This is one of the areas where the teacher acts as a "balancer." There is a sensitive balance between the lovely sense of security that routine can provide and the monotony that can creep in when that routine is unlivened and unleavened. As classes grow comfortable with each other and with the basic format of Morning Meeting, we must introduce variation.

Ruth Charney speaks about the perils of overscriptedness: "Sometimes I build Morning Meeting primarily around a game, after a quick greeting. Or I might stress discussion about current events my students are clearly interested in. Our students are all differently abled and they shine in different parts of Meeting. I find that once a group is comfortable with the order and structure of Morning Meeting, then varying the pace, tempo, and proportion of structures is essential lest comfort turn to complacency, or worse yet, contempt."

Q. *Children in my classroom usually choose to sit next to their friends. Any ideas for making this work better?*

A. Calling this to students' attention, within the context of the larger purposes of Morning Meeting, is often enough intervention. "I notice," says the teacher, "that for the last several mornings, many of us have been choosing to sit next to our good friends. Remember that one of the purposes of Morning Meeting is to help us get to know and feel comfortable with everyone—including those who are not already our friends. Think about that when you choose where you will sit this morning at Meeting." Tying what may seem a superficial detail to the grander vision we hold, to the underlying significance, helps students see why it merits attention.

Sometimes formalizing these expectations into seating cues is necessary. "Boys next to girls" and "new friends' day" can be useful shorthand for reminding students of our expectations and shaping the options a bit, when needed.

There are also ways to arrange seating which engineer different mixes and shake up entrenched patterns. In some primary classes, students make and decorate "sit-upons" with their names, which teachers rotate often so that children sit next to many class members. In older classes, you might want to start with a round of "A Warm Wind Blows" *(Appendix F)*, a very quick game which will shake up the seating arrangement.

Fine Tunings

At certain developmental stages, issues of gender and friendship are at the fore. Recently, I visited in a fifth/sixth grade classroom where the students assembled themselves into a Meeting circle that was a clear sociogram. Girls sat next to girls and boys next to boys. A couple of clear "best friend" clusters could be identified by the shoulder-to-shoulder huddled posture they assumed. The circle was ragged, with two children sitting considerably back from the rest.

The teacher took his place in the circle and looked around quietly. "Meeting seating, please," he announced, and as if they were accomplished square dancers responding to a call, the students arose and wound their way around and across the circle, pausing to survey the scene before sitting again, cross-legged, on the floor. The circle was now a circle, students sitting boy-girl-boy-girl evenly distributed around its perimeter. "Good Morning!" smiled their teacher and the Meeting began.

Scripted? Certainly. But sometimes it's our job to provide a script when the one the students have created is destructive to the group. After an initial and mandatory groan, these students didn't object. They were testing a limit and were relieved to find that, yes, it was still there. There are some ages at which this structure would not be necessary and some ages at which it would not be tolerated and would cause a reaction more problematic than helpful. For that particular group, at that point in their development, it was just right.

Q. *In my classroom, there is a child nobody wants to sit next to. How should I address this?*

A. Frequently students deliberately ostracize a certain child, the social outcast of the group, by not sitting next to her. Action is required on two fronts—one immediate, the other longer term.

First, do whatever you must to stop the exclusion-by-seating. Remove the element of choice by assigning seating patterns that rotate (see previous question).

Or assign partners who will sit together at Morning Meeting and work together during any partner activities within the Meeting.

Identifying why the particular child is not accepted and working with her and others in the group to change the situation is clearly a long-term project. Sometimes, assigning or reading a book chosen for its relevant plot can help prompt a "safe" discussion of a social issue such as exclusion.

Helping a child overcome this kind of reputation, especially when there is a long and entrenched history, is tough. Making sure that all classroom members include her respectfully in the seating and other routines of Morning Meeting is an important start.

Q. *What is the difference between Class Meeting and Morning Meeting?*

A. Class Meetings are held for the purpose of solving a problem, or perhaps planning for a project or event or debriefing afterwards. They are generally not held every day.

Morning Meetings are held for the purposes named earlier and are held every day. They are not used as a time to solve problems or take care of general classroom business. Teachers who use both kinds of meetings often comment that many of the habits of participation and social skills that are developed through Morning Meeting help their students in democratic, cooperative processes like Class Meetings.

Q. *Is it important that I do the components in the order you suggest?*

A. Yes. The order of the four components—Greeting, Sharing, Group Activity, and Morning Message—matters (although they are introduced in a different order, as covered earlier). Greeting serves as a logical warm-up and tone-setter for Sharing, which requires that students feel a sense of comfort and trust in the group. The group must be feeling settled and calm in order for Sharing to work well. We've often seen teachers do Sharing after the Group Activity or Morning Message and then wonder why the students weren't able to listen well or ask focused and thoughtful questions.

The Group Activity follows Sharing because at this point in the Meeting the children are ready for the liveliness which whole-group involvement brings. Morning Message helps to bring the group back to a more calm stance after the liveliness of Activity and serves as a transition to the rest of the school day.

Greeting

Good Morning, Morgan." Hector speaks seriously and earnestly, for that is who Hector is. He looks directly at Morgan, who sits on his left, and offers his right hand.

"Good Morning, Hector!" returns Morgan. He grins widely and grasps Hector's hand with exuberance. Morgan's "Good mornings" are always punctuated with invisible exclamation points, for that is who Morgan is.

Shannon, on Morgan's left, shifts a bit and sits up taller, ready to receive the enthusiasm of a greeting, Morgan-style. And here it comes. "Good Morning, Shannon!" "Good Morning, Morgan!" Her teacher smiles, pleased with Shannon's strong voice and firm handshake. Shannon had entered the third grade classroom in September with a tentative air. Everything about her seemed designed to help her escape the notice of her peers—the acceptable, regulation clothes in quiet colors, her fade-into-the-chair posture, her barely audible voice at Meetings. Now, four months and more than seventy Morning Meetings later, here she is, wearing a smile almost as broad as Morgan's above her bright purple-and-red-striped turtleneck, her hand extended and waiting for his.

And so it goes around the circle. Greeting takes slightly less than three minutes. Every member of the circle—children, teacher, assistant teacher, and Matthew's mother, who is visiting this morning—has been greeted by name, with a handshake and eye contact.

PURPOSES AND REFLECTIONS

Morning Meetings begin with Greeting. Even on days when there isn't time for a full Morning Meeting, teachers convene the circle and make sure Greeting takes place. It is that important because of the tone it sets and the way that tone carries into the rest of the day.

Some mornings, the greeting is basic and straightforward. Variations might be simple, such as students tossing a ball to the student whom they are greeting or substituting a "high five" for the handshake. Other mornings, the greeting process is more elaborate or complex, perhaps fanciful. It might be a call-and-response greeting or a greeting that requires students to offer an adjective describing themselves and beginning with the same letter as their name. Some greetings work with all ages; others have features that make them appropriate only for younger grades or have complex steps better suited to older students.

Long or short, dignified or playful, greetings share four common purposes which are explored in the sections which follow.

Purposes of Greeting

- **Sets a positive tone**

- **Provides a sense of recognition and belonging**

- **Helps children learn names**

- **Gives practice in offering hospitality**

Greeting sets a positive tone for the classroom and the day.

To greet, according to Webster, is to "salute or welcome in a friendly and respectful way." Welcoming, friendly, respectful—those are attributes which characterize the climate in exemplary classrooms. Beginning Morning Meeting with Greeting helps create such a climate.

The fact that there is a designated greeting each day is important. Though there is great room for individual personality to infuse the greeting—Hector's "Good morning" is different from Morgan's which is different from Shannon's—there is also an equity and a safety in having a structure for the

Greeting can be simple and straightforward.
Here, kindergartners pass a greeting around the circle.

greeting. It is unlike the spontaneous, informal way we offer greetings based on our immediate feelings: our close friends get warm smiles; acquaintances get more neutral hellos; those with whom we struggle to get along may get only a perfunctory nod. The goal in Morning Meeting Greeting is for *all* to greet and be greeted equally. Within a classroom community, starting a day by hearing your name spoken with respect and warmth is not a privilege that lands upon just the popular few—those social successes who seem born knowing which T-shirts with what logos are in this year, knowing how to say "Hey…" with just the right inflection and number of syllables instead of "Hi." It is, instead, a right to which all are entitled. When we make time for Greeting every morning, no matter how full the schedule, we make a statement as teachers that we expect respect and equity and that we will do our best to make sure it happens.

Being greeted provides a sense of recognition and belonging which meets a universal human need.

In *The Fifth Discipline Fieldbook* (Senge 1994, 3), Peter Senge tells of the most common greeting among the tribes of Natal in South Africa. The greeting, Sawa Bona, translates literally as "I see you." The standard reply is Sikhona, literally "I am here." The order of these phrases is important and not variable. One cannot be there until one is seen. The truth of this extends beyond linguistic convention.

My student Sue (whom you met in the *Introduction*) went ungreeted and unseen for seven–eighths of her day. Unseen, she felt she was not there. Because she was old enough to do something about it, she chose to physically remove herself. Sadly, our classrooms have too many other children who, though physically present, walk through their days feeling unacknowledged and unseen, feeling they aren't really there.

I think of the old expression "neither here nor there." It means "unimportant and irrelevant," the opposite of how we want our students to feel. We want them to feel important and relevant. We want them to be "here." And so they must feel seen. The act of intentional greeting helps us to see and be seen.

Purposes and Reflections

Greeting helps children learn and use each other's names.

To know someone's name and to feel comfortable using it provides powerful options. It lets us call upon each other. It is a way we get each other's attention, enabling us to ask a question, to recognize one another in a discussion, to request help, to offer congratulations or whisper an apology.

Greeting can also be more elaborate or complex, perhaps even fanciful. Here, a group of fourth graders tries out a puppet greeting.

We can't assume that because students are grouped together they will learn each other's names. Last year a colleague returned from meeting with a group of middle school teachers who had asked him to come and speak with them about *Responsive Classroom* strategies at the middle school level. With fewer than two hundred students comprising the seventh and eighth grades, this regional school was not large, though students from several adjacent towns met for the first time in seventh grade. The faculty wanted to build a sense of community among their students and teachers and had been using a heterogeneous team-based approach to organize their school for several years.

One of the teachers mentioned in conversation that just the day before he had asked a student in his math class to hand back a set of papers and she couldn't do it. Why? She didn't know all of her classmates' names, couldn't match the names at the top of the papers with the faces of her peers. It was mid-January and this was a team of students who had been together in many classes using cooperative learning strategies since September.

A student who doesn't know her classmates well enough to hand them their work is unlikely to feel familiar enough with them to offer her dissenting opinion about a character in a short story or admit that she doesn't quite get this business of "3 is to 21 as x is to 28" or share a poem she wrote about her grandmother. And what a loss that is for her and for her classmates.

Much of our learning happens through social interaction. Knowing names is a fundamental building block for those interactions. It is why name tags at workshops are such a help and one of the reasons why substitute teachers, faced with twenty-five students they may have never seen before and cannot address by name, often feel so powerless. Naming is often the beginning of knowing.

Hearing our name is also a reminder of our identity, our individuality within the group. As members of a community, we regularly identify with larger groups. For example, Center School students are all "Center Schoolers" at their weekly All-School Meeting when they cheer for their soccer team, and they are members of a smaller group, such as the Prime Reds, at the end of the meeting when classes are dismissed one-by-one. Although it's important to feel a part of this larger community, it's also essential to retain a sense of individuality as well. Hearing our name lets us know that someone values speaking to us as an individual and wants our attention. Our name allows us to claim authorship when we are proud of what we have created, a stamp that lets the world know we exist and that what we have done is important.

Only one word or phrase names and identifies each of us as an individual. When my son went to preschool, he was one of three Bens in a class of twelve. When someone called "Hey, Ben!" from the snack table, three boys would respond. None of them wished to be a Benjie or a Benjamin, so they quickly became Ben K, Ben G, and Ben P. Two years later, about to enter kindergarten, Ben wondered aloud, "Think I'll be the only Ben in my new class?" He arrived home after the first day to tell me that things had improved a little. There were only two Bens in this class. He remained Ben K and it became so ingrained in his identity that my Mother's Day cards were signed "Ben K" for years.

Greeting gives children a chance to practice the art of offering hospitality.

Purposes and Reflections

"Hospitality is always an act that benefits the host even more than the guest. The concept of hospitality arose in ancient times when this reciprocity was easier to see: in nomadic cultures, the food and shelter one gave to a stranger yesterday is the food and shelter one hopes to receive from a stranger tomorrow. By offering hospitality, one participates in the endless reweaving of a social fabric on which all can depend." (Palmer 1998, 50)

Welcoming each other to our classroom every day is an act of hospitality. The offering of that welcome, one to another, affirms that we are caretakers of each other in that community. Being a host also implies, builds, and strengthens a person's ownership and investment in that place.

We practice daily the skills of welcoming each other—the clear voice, the friendly smile, the careful remembering that Nicholas likes to be called Nick, the firm handshake. When guests visit and are part of our circle, we extend a welcome to them as well, although it can feel a bit awkward at first. "Should we call her Carol or Mrs. DiAngelo?" whispers Andy to his teacher when he notices that his friend Matt's mother is coming to Morning Meeting. "Could you check with her and see which would feel more comfortable to her?" replies his teacher.

Several important messages are conveyed in this suggestion. First, there is no one right answer to that question in our culture these days. Some parents prefer that children use their first names; others deem it disrespectful. Second, the role of a host is to make the guest feel respected and comfortable. And third, asking a polite and direct question is a fine way to get an answer you need. It is practice in assertiveness seasoned with courtesy, not an easy blend to get right at any age.

Kindergarten teacher Eileen Mariani of Erving Elementary School in Millers Falls, Massachusetts, is proud of a January morning in her room.

These fifth graders practice the skills of "respectful" greeting:
making eye contact, shaking hands gently,
saying the person's name clearly.

The habit of greeting within the Morning Meeting circle had been well established. On that particular morning it was Isaac's turn to be Morning Meeting leader. Isaac was a shy boy who approached his role as leader with some trepidation. Eileen watched carefully, ready to help if Isaac seemed worried at any point. But, no need, he was doing splendidly.

He had chosen "Good Morning, Friends" (Appendix E) for the greeting and it had been clapped and stamped with a nicely modulated glee around the circle, just returning to Isaac, when Isaac glanced up and stood abruptly, heading for the door. Eileen, whose view of the door was blocked by a bookshelf, also rose to survey what was going on. There stood Isaac, framed by the doorway, hand extended to a distinguished-looking visitor who was entering the room with the principal. "Good morning, Mr….Uh…I'm sorry, what is your name please?" Isaac proceeded to shake the visitor's hand before walking gravely back to his place on the rug to continue the Meeting.

The months of modeling and practicing, the discussions of "What can you do if you don't remember someone's name?" had taken hold and enabled Isaac to extend graceful hospitality, not just beyond Morning Meeting with class-mates, but even to a stranger at the door. Isaac's extended hand was a true act of welcome and hospitality.

Highlights of Greeting

- **Ensures that every child names and notices others at the outset of the day**

- **Allows the teacher to observe and "take the pulse" of the group that day**

- **Provides practice in elements of greeting such as making eye contact and shaking hands**

- **Requires students to extend the range of classmates they spontaneously notice and greet**

- **Helps students to reach across gender, clique, and friendship lines that form at particular ages**

- **Can employ strategies which challenge the intellect (patterns, acquisition of foreign language phrases, set making)**

- **Encourages clear and audible speech**

Purposes and Reflections

Getting Started

You may want to browse through or study *Appendix E,* which lists and describes a wide range of greetings, to get a sense of their variety and content before continuing on to the next section.

GETTING STARTED

Begin by introducing Greeting.

Choosing your language carefully when introducing Greeting establishes expectations from the outset. "We are going to learn to do lots of different friendly and respectful greetings," states the teacher, before going on to model what she means by those two adjectives.

The teacher turns to Sara and greets her, then asks the class, "What did you notice?"

"You said her name."

"You looked at her."

"You took her hand."

"Sara, what did you notice about the way I held your hand?"

Specific behaviors are noted and named, becoming part of a classroom lexicon. You might write on the chart as you summarize, "So, a friendly greeting means saying a person's name, looking at the person, and shaking hands in a gentle way."

As always, language and focus will vary with the age of the children in the group. With older children, focusing on the "respectful" aspect is often more useful. Even the most entrenched adolescents who argue that their choice of friends is their own business will acknowledge that all of us are entitled to respectful treatment.

Always begin by modeling and practicing the positive ways of greeting. Then, depending on the make-up of your class, you may want to insert some of the more subtle gestures that children frequently try out. You might mumble a person's name, pump a hand exaggeratedly, or look at the clock while greeting a child. "How did I or didn't I show respect?" The details matter. We know that; they know that. Modeling and discussion helps them know that we know.

Greeting

Keep Greeting simple at first.

When first introducing Greeting to a group, or at the year's start when a new group is getting to know each other, simple, direct greetings work best. The teacher models "greeting," calling attention to important qualities of the greeting—names spoken clearly, greeter and greeted looking directly at each other, friendly handshakes and voices. When students are able to fluently go around the circle saying "Good morning" to each other, then it's time to introduce various other greetings *(Appendix E)*.

This example illustrates how Sandra Norried (Ms. N.) of Washington, DC, a masterful and experienced third grade teacher, offers her class just the right amount of choice.

For the first weeks of school, Ms. N. has chosen the greeting and now, in October, is beginning to hand that choice over to students. She knows from her years of teaching, however, that too many choices can be as limiting as too few, especially when the year is young. So for this week, the leader will not choose the greeting itself, but one element of it—a rhythm instrument. Each instrument has been introduced, one per day, and now there are six to choose from.

"Today Sienna will lead our greeting. Sienna, what will you use?"

Ms. N. hands Sienna a blue crate containing an assortment of rhythm instruments. Sienna studies the possibilities intently for a moment before reaching in to make her choice. Gently, with the slightest of jingles, she produces a tambourine and holds it aloft for her classmates to see. A collective grin spreads around the circle. The tambourine is clearly a favorite of these third graders.

The greeting moves clockwise around the circle. After each "Good morning," the greeter shakes the tambourine before passing it to the greeted. Some shake it tentatively and softly; others brandish it above their heads, with extended and elaborated rhythms involving their whole bodies.

Getting Started

This kind of boundary-setting helps to define space for learning, something teachers do constantly in their planning—deciding how far apart to place the cones on the play yard for tag games, which books to set out on the Choice Reading Shelf, how many choices to make available for greetings. Ideally, we set boundaries far enough apart that they allow ample room for exploration and experimentation, but not so wide that they allow students to get lost.

Help students learn each others' names.

Name tags, either prepared ahead by the teacher or made by students, are a great help in the early days of a new group. There are also many games and activities which focus upon learning names *(Appendices E and F)* and are very helpful in the early days. With young children, starting the year with chorus greetings in which everyone says or sings the names together can help the children feel comfortable and help them learn each others' names. When the children are ready to say names individually, making pairs ahead of Greeting so that each is prepared to say a partner's name can help boost children's confidence.

Anticipate and help students handle awkward moments.

Many greetings require students to choose the person they will greet, rather than simply proceeding around the circle in order. This requires participants to pay attention in order to remember who has and hasn't been named. Teachers can help by modeling what to do in those inevitable moments when, despite their best efforts, students can't remember a name or who has already been greeted. "What can you say if you forget someone's name?" "What can you say if you forget who has been greeted?" Some teachers work out a signal—such as thumbs up until you're greeted—with their class. Such signals help the last few greeters who may be struggling to remember who remains to be greeted.

Greeting responsibilities

In implementing and assessing Greeting, keep the following general responsibilities in mind.

Teachers' responsibilities

- **Teach a variety of age-appropriate greetings**

- **Model aspects of warm and respectful greeting**

- **Make sure children use friendly and appropriate words and body language**

- **Give students opportunities to choose and lead greetings**

Greeting

Students' responsibilities

- **Choose different classmates each day to greet**

- **Wait for their turn to greet**

- **Use a clear, audible voice**

- **Use friendly and appropriate body language and tone of voice**

FINE TUNINGS

Q. *Do I need to do Greeting every single day? What about days when we have no time, when the music teacher is waiting for my class or we're going on a field trip and we need to leave right away?*

A. Greeting, even once the group is well established, is important to do every single day. Once the group is in the habit of forming the Morning Meeting circle, a very quick greeting can be done in virtually no time. One class at Greenfield Center School has invented a greeting for just such no-time days. It is called "Lefty-Righty" *(Appendix E)* and has become a favorite of the class. Practice it first on a day when you are not rushed to see if it appeals to you.

For the "Tuesday-is-Art-right-away" situation, where the time crunch will be regular, you might suggest that the art teacher join your class for five minutes to be part of Greeting before beginning the art lesson.

Another approach is to do Greeting after your class reconvenes. For example, on field trips teachers sometimes gather students after reaching their destination for a brief check-in and a condensed Meeting with a simple greeting.

Q. *What about the child who just can't speak in front of the group? How can I help him participate in Greeting?*

Fine Tunings

A. This is not uncommon, particularly with five-year-olds, though some children are painfully shy at older ages as well. As the question implies, it is important to find a way to make sure that these children are part of the routine.

It is helpful to approach this from two angles. First, find a way to help the child participate. Sometimes practicing with the child individually before Meeting, making sure that he knows whom he will greet, helps. Elisabeth Olivera, teacher in a bilingual kindergarten in Holyoke, Massachusetts, suggests that the teacher and student say the words together, with the teacher gradually softening her voice until the child is able to speak on his own.

Second, in your role as interpreter, help the group understand what is going on and how they can be helpful. The explanation should be simple and matter-of-fact: "Terry doesn't want to talk in Meeting yet, but I hope that he will find his words soon. Until he does, you can help by making sure he is greeted and I will help by greeting the next person with him."

This is a wonderful opportunity to validate that it is acceptable, not shameful, for members of the group to struggle sometimes, that we all have our struggles with different activities, and that we can help each other through those struggles with acceptance and encouragement.

Q. *My students seem to be getting bored with Greeting.*

A. Variety is important to keep routines from getting stale and this is certainly true of Greeting. There is a fine balance between the comfort and pleasure that predictable, familiar structures bring and the boredom that can pervade the group when there are no changes in format or tempo.

When the mood is boredom, it's time for variation. Introducing new greetings can happen at any time in the year. Students often come up with clever adaptations to old favorites. I think of the Elbow Rock Greeting *(Appendix E)* which I saw in Kensington School in Springfield, Massachusetts, where fourth grade students had invented an "armshake" in which they extended right arms, bent at the elbow, and shook arms rather than hands. There are plenty of greetings to choose from in *Appendix E.* As a reminder of the possibilities, teachers often post a chart that lists the class repertoire of greetings.

It's also important to search for the source of the boredom. Perhaps it is a simple monotony stemming from the same old greeting activities and it's time to introduce some additional choices. Or perhaps the class is turning a developmental corner and greetings that were safe and right for your mostly sevens are feeling too narrow for your burgeoning eight-year-olds, who crave some sanctioned ways to vent their boisterous side.

Q. *I teach in the upper grades and my students usually start out fine with Greeting. However, as the year goes on, they tend to get sloppy and silly. They complain that it's babyish and that they know everyone's names and don't see why they have to keep doing this.*

A. This is not an unusual occurrence, particularly with older children as they get used to Morning Meeting, comfortable with the class, and lax with expectations. When you see children getting sloppy with Greeting, it's time to stop the Meeting. Whispering, nudging, in-jokes, fake smiles, and muffled names are all good reasons to stop a Meeting. When these occur, it's a signal that the class has lost sight of the real purpose behind Greeting and they need some help to get back on track.

A reminder of the purpose behind greetings may be in order. Remind the group that greetings welcome and acknowledge people in the community and that a proper greeting is a vital part of the well-being of the group that day. Emphasize that greeting one another is important work; it is not simply an amusement. Sometimes sharing a story with the students, such as the one offered earlier about Sue (who never felt acknowledged) or the story of a time when you, as an adult, felt unnoticed helps to remind children of the importance of what they are doing. A discussion about how a sincere versus an insincere greeting really feels may also be helpful. You might ask the children for suggestions of ways to make Greeting work better while also insisting that they greet each other correctly.

Greeting

Q. *Students always choose their friends to greet first, and the least popular are always left until last to be greeted. How can I address this without embarrassing individuals?*

A. It is important for students to learn to greet all members of the class in a friendly and interested way. We expect students to say "Good morning" to a variety of classmates, not simply their best friends. Almost always, this requires acknowledging and naming this expectation. "If Morning Meeting is a time when we get to know people that we don't usually work or play with, then who might we say 'Good morning' to?" Or, "Today, before we begin Greeting, I want each of us to look around the circle and think of someone we might greet whom we haven't greeted yet this week."

Fine Tunings

Issues of gender, cliques, and best friends, while present to some degree at most age levels, are developmental milestones of nine-to-thirteen-year-olds and can manifest themselves with considerable ferocity during those stages. Greeting can help students work on these issues within the safety of teacher-imposed structures.

Q. *Some of the behaviors we teach in Morning Meeting, such as making eye contact and smiling at people they don't know, could get my students in real trouble on the streets where they live. How can we ask them to behave one way in school, another way when they go out the door?*

A. Different cultures do have different rules. The culture in our school may be very different from the culture of a community just a hundred yards away— as different as Nigeria is from Finland. It is very important to acknowledge this and to think through what it means for our students. Not only is it possible for them to understand this, it is essential.

Several years ago, I listened to a panel of wise and experienced principals of urban schools discuss this issue. "From a very early age our children must, and do, differentiate and adapt to the different rules that govern their behavior in the several cultures they inhabit every single day—home, streets, school," stated one.

"I talk about the different hats we all wear, and how we sometimes wear the same hat differently in different places," offered another. "In school, we wear our caps with the visor facing front. When we get ready to go out the door to go home, we stop and turn them around. In the hallways of our school you see a stranger, look him in the eyes, smile, and say 'Good morning.' In the streets you walk to get home, you see a stranger, you avert your eyes and walk on by."

Greeting

Sharing

THE ART OF CARING CONVERSATION

Agreeting has made its way around the circle of fourth graders and Ms. Scamardella glances at the Sharing Board. "Anita, I notice that you signed up for Sharing today."

"This afternoon," announces Anita, "my Grammy's coming home from the hospital." There is a pause while the other students wait to see if more information is coming. Anita, while not exactly shy, is economical with words. Several children raise their hands. Anita chooses to recognize a boy directly across the circle first. "Reginald."

"I hope she gets well quick," he comments. Anita nods and sends a small smile his way, an acknowledgment of his wish.

Two other hands in the circle are raised. "Sharon," says Anita.

"I didn't know that she was in the hospital. Was she sick for a very long time?"

"They took her in on Sunday," responds Anita. "It was scary because she couldn't eat or anything, her stomach hurt so bad. She even cried when they moved her." Faces around the circle are serious as they receive this detail.

Anita surveys the circle. One classmate raises a hand and Anita calls on her. "Raquel."

"I bet you're glad she can come home," offers Raquel.

Anita nods emphatically. "I am, I really am."

PURPOSES AND REFLECTIONS

Sharing follows Greeting in Morning Meeting. It is a structure in which students present news they wish to share and respond to each other by asking questions and offering comments.

Anita's sharing and her classmates' responses reveal a skilled use of verbal communication and an underlying attitude of care. The teacher didn't just get lucky and inherit a class of nine- and ten-year-olds gifted in these ways. She and the teachers of earlier grades in her school teach this behavior and encourage this attitude. They do this, of course, all through the day and all through their curriculum, but one of the times when it is a primary focus is Sharing in Morning Meeting.

Purposes and Reflections

Purposes of Sharing

- **Helps develop the skills of caring communication and involvement with one another**

- **Extends the knowing and being known that is essential for the development of community and for individuals' sense of significance**

- **Encourages habits of inquiry and thought important for cognitive growth**

- **Provides practice in speaking to a group in a strong and individual voice**

- **Strengthens vocabulary development and reading success**

Sharing helps develop the skills of caring communication and involvement with one another.

In *The Challenge to Care in Schools,* Nel Noddings offers a clear and instructive exploration of the concept of caring as dependent on the relationship between two people. (Noddings 1992, 15–16) She defines a caring relationship as a connection or encounter between two human beings—a "carer" and a "cared-for" who must both contribute in certain ways. If either party fails, then there may

Sharing helps children learn about each others' interests
and lives outside of school.

still be a relationship, but it is not a caring one. The carer must be receptive and attentive to the cared-for and must feel the desire to help the other. The cared-for must receive the act of caring and recognize it by a response.

Sharing in Morning Meeting is the application of this construct, its details translated so that they can be understood and appreciated by five-year-olds and nine-year-olds and fourteen-year-olds. Through modeling, discussion, and practice of their different responsibilities as a sharer and a member of the audience, students develop their understanding of the roles of cared-for and carer and their capacity to assume them.

Eleven-year-old Hallie shares. "Today after school my mother is taking me to the hospital and I'm gonna' bring cards I made to people there. I'm ready for questions and comments."

"Do you want any of us to sign them?"

"Sure. Anybody who wants to."

"I think it's nice of you to do that, to make those cards."

"Thank you."

It is a simple, brief exchange in which both carers and cared-for are performing fluently. Implicit in the first question is a compliment: this is a project that sounds so good I'd like to be part of it. In granting permission, Hallie receives and responds to this offering of care, just as she does to the next comment, a more direct compliment.

It doesn't always go so smoothly, of course.

"We got a new puppy this weekend," shares kindergartner Tessa. "I'm ready for questions and comments." Hands shoot up around the circle. "Allie."

"I have a dog, too, and this morning he threw up on his rug," begins Allie, taking a breath as she prepares to launch into her tale.

Her teacher takes advantage of the pause. "Tomorrow when it's your turn to share you can tell us about your dog. Right now, can you think of a question or a comment for Tessa about her news?"

Reminded, Allie certainly can. "What does your puppy look like?" And Sharing is back on track.

Purposes and Reflections

Sharing extends the knowing and being known that is essential for the development of community and for individuals' sense of significance.

While Greeting helps everyone know the names of the members of the classroom community, Sharing builds on that knowledge by helping children know the people attached to the names. As we offer information, we learn about each other—whose grandpa just moved in because he's getting so forgetful, who owns a boa constrictor, who loves Matt Christopher books, and who goes to the YMCA every day after school. Sharing helps build a transition between home and school.

Sometimes Sharing is structured by a particular topic. "This week we will each share something interesting we learned from the biographies we are reading," assigns the teacher, or "This week Sharing will be about something you made." Although the Sharing topic is focused, sharers reveal unique and individual information nonetheless.

Often the revelations help establish a common ground between students that is carried beyond the Meeting. Consulting teacher Marlynn Clayton, skilled teacher of young children, notes that she frequently helps children spot the connection and extend it. "There isn't time for more comments in Sharing, but maybe the three of you could have lunch together and talk more about your baseball card collections," she might suggest.

This kind of gentle guidance helps students move beyond their existing circle of friends. Left to our own devices, we often spend time with those with whom we are most comfortable, those most "like us," which limits our growth. Sharing allows students to begin with a common interest, a starting place from which to learn about differences as well as similarities. The richest communication requires both acknowledgment of common ground and ability to explore differences in perspective and ideas.

Sharing which lets every member of the community hear and be heard demands an engagement that stretches our understanding and rewards us all.

Sharing encourages habits of inquiry and thought important for cognitive growth.

The research of many respected educational theorists, including Piaget and Vygotsky, has examined and documented the relationship between social context and cognitive development. (Rogoff 1990, 192) Though Piaget and Vygotsky each describe different models for the ways in which social interaction influences cognitive development, both recognize the importance of developing the following skills:

Sharing

- Stating one's thoughts with clarity
- Listening actively and forming questions that clarify
- Seeing things from another's perspective

The practice of sharing and responding during Morning Meeting nourishes these important cognitive skills.

Stating one's thoughts with clarity

In order to present a piece of news to classmates, students must be able to craft a comprehensible narration and deliver it. If it is not clear, the feedback will be immediate.

"Wait a minute. I'm confused. Was it your brother or your father who forgot to pick you up last night?" Todd asks his classmate, Michael, after a rambling and confused story. It is a genuine question; Todd wants to understand and respond to Michael's experience.

Listening actively and forming questions that clarify

Active listening is motivated by the expectation that each student's job is to formulate a question that elicits more information or to make a comment that shows interest in the news presented or concern for the sharer. When students accept these responsibilities, they listen carefully and remember well, habits important for every learner.

To further promote good listening, particularly in earlier grades, teachers will sometimes ask questions at the end of Sharing that test the group's ability to recall details. "Who can remember the name of Leanne's turtle?" "What was the name of the fruit Marisa brought in?"

Seeing things from another's perspective

Sheldon Berman, co-founder of Educators for Social Responsibility, stated in a recent address that taking another's perspective "is the linchpin in the development of social consciousness. How can we get beyond ourselves, know what's going on for another person? That's where social responsibility begins." (Berman 1998)

Comments which respond to Sharing require seeing things from another's perspective. Commenting well entails understanding another person's situation, feelings, and motives. Whether the sharing is about something momentous or the everyday stuff of our lives, responding well requires stepping outside our own vantage point to try and imagine how another person feels or regards something.

"I bet you feel really happy that you can get your cast taken off tomorrow."

"I think the way you made the orange and the red blur together in your painting really looks like fire."

"I hope your cat will be all right."

All are statements informed by empathy, by that ability to "get beyond ourselves" which Berman notes. They are comments that say "I listened to you. I care about how you feel."

Sharing provides practice in speaking to a group in a strong and individual voice.

Many adults share a deep apprehension, ranging from nervousness to utter terror, at the thought of speaking to a group. In my own school experience, we spoke to a group only in formal and artificial situations, seldom on anything we really knew about or of deep interest to us. Instead, we were assigned to do "Oral Reports" on designated topics, reports that were thinly disguised paraphrases of encyclopedia passages. Grades were correlated to the length of time we spoke, rather than the content. It took at least five horrifying minutes to get an "A" in seventh grade English class. Mumbling helped disguise the fact that we couldn't pronounce a third of the words we had painstakingly copied.

How blessedly different Sharing is! First of all, the material has intrinsic interest and students can make choices even within structured topics. A student assigned to share news "that shows courage" has many choices. Will she share about her seventy-two-year-old grandmother, always terrified of the water, who is now bravely taking beginner's swimming lessons? Or will she share a story she saw on television's evening news about firefighters who rescued three people from a downtown apartment fire last night?

Also, one of our jobs as sharer is to keep our presentation brief and understandable rather than padding it to stretch it out. When others are listening and want to respond, they will not allow us to mumble or to speak in those rapid, inaudible monotones, which were the style in my seventh-grade class. The chance to practice is frequent, brief, informal (yet structured), and unjudged by letter grades.

Sharing

Sharing strengthens vocabulary development and reading success.

The Home-School Study of Language and Literacy Development is a longitudinal study investigating the links between early oral language development of children and their literacy success in elementary and middle school. One of the findings is that opportunities for children to participate in "interesting conversations with adults" are strongly related to children's reading success in school. The study found that it is important for children to engage regularly in "conversation that goes beyond the here and now, and which relies on language to convey images and information about other times and places. A girl describing a recent trip to the zoo over dinner, for example, would rely on her decontextualized language skills to describe what she had seen." (Lynn 1997, 2) This is exactly the kind of conversation that takes place during Sharing.

As students work at expressing themselves and understanding others through conversation, the process is filled with opportunities for vocabulary enrichment. In the context of the "real" conversations in Sharing, teachers may use words and terms that are unfamiliar to students and correct students' misunderstandings of vocabulary.

Consider this scene from a third grade classroom I visited recently. It was Regina's turn to share.

"On Saturday I went to Adventure World with my uncle. I went swimming there and I drowned," states Regina.

Her classmates are full of questions about her trip. The first questions seek to establish the logistics of her trip.

"What parts of Adventure World did you go to?"

"How long did it take to get there?"

"Was there traffic?"

Then comes a question that moves past the details to the core of her sharing. "Was it scary when you drowned?"

Wide-eyed and solemn, Regina nods emphatically. "It was really scary."

Her teacher has listened and observed intently during these exchanges. She notices that all of the children understand Regina's news and they all share the same misunderstanding.

"Regina," she asks, "when you said that you drowned, did you mean that you had trouble swimming in the water?"

Regina nods, yes, that's what she meant. An impromptu vocabulary lesson follows, a thread picked up from the fabric of Regina's sharing and woven seamlessly into the classroom circle.

"Drowned is connected to having trouble in the water," affirms the teacher, "but it means that you had so much trouble that you died from not being able to get above the water to breathe."

Purposes and Reflections

After a student has shared, she asks for questions and comments from her classmates.

The class listens intently. There is no embarrassment attached to the mistake; they are glad to receive this information, given crisply and matter-of-factly. It extends their ability to describe their own experiences and to interpret the experiences of others accurately in both oral and written communications.

Highlights of Sharing

- **Provides an arena for students to share news**

- **Helps students develop the ability to gauge the appropriateness of sharing various kinds of news with different audiences**

- **Allows students to practice framing constructive, purposeful questions**

- **Helps students develop a repertoire of responses to different kinds of news**

- **Develops good oral communication skills—both presentation skills and listening skills**

- **Lets students learn information about each other**

- **Enhances vocabulary development and reading success**

- **Offers practice in speaking to a group**

- **Gives practice in considering others' perspectives, developing empathy and social consciousness**

- **Empowers students by letting them run their sharing**

Sharing

GETTING STARTED

Introduce Sharing.

Sharing is usually the last component of Morning Meeting to be introduced, after Greeting, Group Activity, and Morning Message have been introduced and

*Children listen more carefully to the sharing when they
are expected to formulate good questions and comments.*

established. (See *Fine Tunings* section of the chapter, *"Morning Meeting: An
Overview,"* for a review of the issues involved in the order of components.)

Introduce Sharing by explaining its purpose and structure. "One of the purposes of Morning Meeting is to help us get to know each other better. Each day
in our Morning Meeting there will be a time for some of us to share news about
things in our lives with the class. Everyone will get a chance to share, though
usually not every day."

In this introduction, brainstorm with children appropriate things to share,
making sure that events and information are included, not just objects. Ideas will
vary with different ages, of course. This introductory session is a time to generate ideas with a broad scope of possible topics; unless an idea for something to
share is conspicuously inappropriate, it is not a time to limit or refine notions
about sharing. That will evolve as sharing is practiced.

Discuss and model the "jobs" of the sharer.

The "jobs" of the sharer include using a voice that is strong and clear and sharing news that is brief and focused. "I'm going to share," begins the teacher,
"about something that I saw while driving to school this morning. I had to stop
and wait because twelve wild turkeys were in the middle of the road, just milling
around. They didn't seem to even notice my car." He calls upon his students to

note that his voice is strong and clear and his news brief and focused and reminds them to think about those "jobs" when it is their turn to share.

When your students are preparing for their first sharings early in the year, you may want to assign each sharer a partner who will listen to the sharing ahead of time and give feedback based on the defined "jobs" of the sharer.

- Did the sharer use a strong voice?

- Was the news short and clear?

Children sometimes need help focusing their sharing. It is often hard for them to select the most important things, rather than tell everything. "Tell one important part of your visit to the zoo," can be helpful. Some teachers, particularly of younger children or of children who want to tell "breakfast-to-bed" stories, use a "two sentence rule" as a sharing guideline. Sometimes, however, when the speaker just can't stop rambling, the teacher must interrupt. "You've told us lots of interesting things about your team, Sara. Let's see if there are questions."

Sharing

Discuss and model good questions and comments.

Audience members have two important jobs. First, they must listen carefully to the sharer. Second, they must respond with respectful, caring questions and comments.

Good questions

What is a good question? Good questions show a genuine interest in the sharer and her news. They can inquire about the factual or emotional content of a sharing and get information that extends understanding about what has been shared. Sometimes a question clarifies information. Good questions are often open-ended, requiring more than just a yes-or-no response from the sharer.

Good questions reflect the spirit of Sharing—the sharer is acknowledged, noticed, and encouraged. What might be a wonderful question in a debate club—challenging and argumentative, designed to exhibit the knowledge of the questioner—is an unacceptable question in Sharing.

Good questioning skills can be practiced quite deliberately. After sharing about his turkey sighting, the teacher says to the class, "Today we're going to practice asking good questions. Your questions might ask about something that you didn't understand. They might ask for more information about what I told you or they might ask how I felt about it."

"How big were the turkeys?"

"What did they look like?"

"Were you worried that you might hit one?"

"Why do you think they were in the road?"

"How did you get them to move out of the road?"

A specific kind of question-asking skill may be isolated and practiced, also. "Today I want each person to think of a question about my sharing that cannot be answered by just yes or no."

Good comments

Good comments notice and appreciate elements of the sharing and keep the focus on the sharer. Laura has brought a photo of her new puppy to share. Interest is high among her classmates; almost everyone has a hand raised. The questions asked are full of real interest and a full picture of this puppy emerges from Laura's answers. It's a girl, she sleeps a lot, eats a lot, and in between she likes to chew things, sometimes things she's not supposed to. The vet thinks she will get to be at least seventy-five pounds and Laura got her from somebody her dad works with whose dog had puppies and needed to find homes for them.

The comments, however, consist entirely of other pet owners' stories. Each one is a variation on the theme of "When I got my dog (hamster, kitten)…" While this would be lovely lunch table conversation, the focus moving from person to person but related to a central topic, it does not fit the guidelines for Sharing comments. A lesson on comments that focus upon the sharer is in order and the teacher decides to capitalize on the eager involvement of the class, directing their interest back to Laura's story.

"I want everyone in the circle to think of a comment that speaks about Laura's news. You might say something that you notice or you might think about how she seems to feel about getting her puppy and comment about that." There is a thoughtful silence as the children sift their ideas through the filters their teacher has named. Slowly the hands go back up.

"I think your puppy looks really sweet."

"I noticed how one ear stands up and one ear doesn't in your picture. I think that's really cute."

"I hope your puppy doesn't chew any more of your shoes."

"I think it's really nice that you took a puppy that might not have had a home otherwise."

"I bet you're really happy to have a puppy."

"Five comments and every one of them was directly connected to Laura's news about her puppy. You really paid attention to Laura," recognizes the teacher.

Set up a system which gives everyone the chance to share.

Most teachers find it helpful to have a sign-up system which ensures that each child is a sharer at least once a week. Children can sign up to share the day before Meeting or that same morning. Another way is to assign each child a regular day for sharing. Limiting the number of questions and comments each sharer can accept helps to keep Sharing moving and feeling equitable.

Make sure to give children the responsibility to conduct their sharing.

Sharing

Let the sharer call on people who have questions and comments. As teachers, we often lead or chair discussions and slide easily into this role during Sharing. Try to be aware of this habit and work on changing to a less directive approach. Sharing will be much more meaningful if children feel a sense of ownership and responsibility for conducting their sharing.

Focus the flow and type of sharing and responses as necessary.

There will be many times when you need to direct the flow because questions and comments are being offered by the same students or certain sharings elicit little response. It is important to address these issues directly, enabling students to think about and practice the skills of conversation involved. It may be time for a refresher course in good questioning or commenting or a review of the sharer's job and some modeling. This differs from earlier modeling because it focuses on a particular aspect of Sharing skills in response to a problem you observe.

Begin by naming what you see as the problem. "I notice," you might say at the next day's Meeting, "that, even though there has been some really interesting sharing, lots of us aren't thinking of questions or comments." Or, "I've been noticing that sometimes when we share, we tell so many details that the audience has a really hard job thinking of anything important to ask."

Then structure an exercise, offering yourself as model, that will address what you have named.

"Listen to my sharing and notice all the facts I've told you. Last night I went to see a play my daughter was in. What facts did you hear?"

"You went to a play."

"Your daughter was in it."

"It was last night."

"What didn't I tell you that you might want to know?"

"What was the name of the play?"

"Was it funny or serious?"

"What was the name of the character your daughter played?"

"Did your daughter remember all her lines?"

"Was it a really long play?" This from Mark, who hates to sit still.

"Where was it? A fancy theater?"

Getting Started

"Wow. You thought of five questions based on a sharing that only told you three facts," I note. "The rest of this week I want our sharers to make sure they tell only a couple of important facts in their sharing, and I want the audience to pay attention to what else it would be interesting to find out."

Don't be afraid to intervene in your role as "guide."

Teachers guide students' participation in the art of caring conversation. "Guided participation," says psychologist Barbara Rogoff, "involves children and their caregivers and companions in the collaborative processes of (1) building

Most teachers find it helpful to have a sign-up system which ensures that each child is a sharer at least once a week.

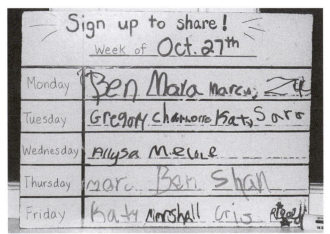

bridges from children's present understanding and skills to reach new understanding and skills, and (2) arranging and structuring children's participation in activities, with dynamic shifts over development in children's responsibilities." (Rogoff 1990, 8)

We all participate in conversations throughout the day. For children, school days should be, and generally are, full of opportunities for conversations. The guided participation of sharing at Morning Meeting, however, has a number of important distinctions from the conversational participation at the water cooler or the sand table. The teacher's role as a guide and the structures of Sharing enable verbal interactions and responses that children may not yet be capable of independently.

This situation came to life for me in a visit to Cynthia Donnelly's first grade classroom in Springfield, Massachusetts.

Sharing

It was December, only a few days before the holiday vacation and these six-year-olds were spilling over with the excitement of the season. Cynthia's understanding of her class and her years of experience were called upon frequently to keep them focused at Morning Meeting.

A hasty version of Speed Ball Greeting had left several children ungreeted, to which Cynthia had responded, "OK, that was just a test run. Now we'll try it again, being speedy and remembering everybody." What a gracious and adept way to demand that they do it right. And do it right they did, beating their prior record of fifty-one seconds, with everyone included.

"Nice job, class," affirmed Cynthia. "Today, Anthony will share first."

Anthony leaned forward eagerly and his words flew out fast and excited. "My grandma's coming from Italy to visit me!"

"He already told us that!" blurted Adam. It was a thoroughly six-year-old retort, brash and impulsive, tinged with righteous indignation at having to hear something twice. It was really not meant to be unkind, though it fell with a cruel thud upon the enthusiastic Anthony. Adam—and a crestfallen Anthony—along with their nineteen classmates, looked to their teacher for a ruling.

But their teacher didn't offer them one. Instead she offered them a question. It was a question that masterfully sidestepped the issue of whether the news had or hadn't been offered before and pointed her students toward a more important issue. "If Anthony already told us his grandma was coming, why might he tell us again? What would make a person repeat news?"

Several ideas were ventured. "I say things twice when I'm really excited!"

"Maybe Anthony's got more to tell than when he told it the first time."

"Probably 'cause it's really important news to you."

Cynthia nodded, receiving these suggestions thoughtfully, before handing the reins back to Anthony. "OK, Anthony, you can choose people for questions and comments." Questions abounded:

"How long since you saw her?"

"When's she coming?"

"Is she gonna bring you a present from Italy?"

Cynthia's hand is up in the air. "Maybe, Anthony, your grandma could come to school with you."

Without the guidance of their teacher, it is unlikely that a group of six-year-olds could have moved beyond their concern about the detail of Adam's observation into a contemplation based upon empathy for Anthony. It is more likely that their diversion into "who said what when" would have prevented them from responding to Anthony's news at all.

Getting Started

This is not to suggest that Cynthia, in the thirty seconds in which she responded to the situation, considered the theoretical foundation and the probable effects of her actions, consciously constructing an opportunity for "guided participation." Construct it she did, however, in a moment infused by a remarkable mix of teacherly instinct and expertise.

The structures and guided aspect of Sharing also allow freedom to fumble and stumble as we learn. Cynthia's intervention and response to Adam's comment let her whole class know that the important thing was to think about Anthony and to respond to his news in a caring way. By not engaging directly with Adam or with the substance of his accusation—whether Anthony had or hadn't shared this already—she let them know that it was not a helpful comment. But she did this in a way that did not highlight Adam or his blunder.

Adam stood corrected, but gently and quickly. In order to learn from our mistakes, the feedback must be clear enough so that we understand what we must try to do differently next time, but not so sharp that we recoil in embarrassment. When our humiliation is large or when we are mired in our own awkwardness with no hand extended to pull us out, we learn defensiveness or avoidance instead of a more positive form of engagement.

Because Sharing is a whole-class activity, there is the potential for all to learn from each interaction. Cynthia invited the whole class to help solve the puzzle of why a person might share old news. In this structure and under her guidance, the discovery was not limited to the two boys directly involved, but became a spontaneous, whole-class lesson in understanding and motivation.

As the class becomes familiar with the basic format of Sharing, give structure to the content as needed.

Sometimes teachers need to take an active role in directing the content of Sharing. I have a painful memory of substituting in a fifth and sixth grade classroom where I did not know the students and their demographics well. It was the day after February vacation and the first three sharings involved the details of expensive ski vacations—the depth of the powder, the temperature in Colorado, the hot springs. Trying desperately to figure out how to redirect this mostly unintentional cruelty, I watched the expressions on the faces of the children who had spent their week at home watching younger siblings or going to the local YMCA program.

Obviously we don't want to stifle children from sharing about special opportunities that come their way. But we do want our classrooms to be places where economic distinctions are not used to oppress. One way we can address this within the context of Sharing is by helping students to identify and share about activities and news which are non-material—which don't involve things or special opportunities based on economics. A post-vacation week sharing topic might be about someone you spent time with during vacation, for example.

In classes of younger children, a variation of the "Luxury Vacation" sharing is the "Bring and Brag" syndrome. Many teachers avoid this by a general "no toys for sharing" rule. Recognizing, however, that sometimes it is important to have a chance to share a special toy, many teachers define a category—category sharing—to allow those opportunities while providing some focus which keeps the emphasis away from the completely materialistic. One week might be "Bring Your Favorite Stuffie Week" or "Bring a Toy You Made Week."

Sometimes teachers use categories simply to give children ideas about different kinds of sharing, such as news about "Grandparents" or "Something You Found in Nature." With older children, sharing focused upon current events is often very successful.

Help students distinguish between news appropriate for classroom sharing and news to be shared just with the teacher.

For the purposes of Morning Meeting, there are two overall categories of news—community news and private family news. Community news is news that is appropriate for the classroom community to hear and private family news

Sharing

is news that is not appropriate for sharing with the whole class. This might be news that is confidential from a legal or ethical viewpoint. It might involve details a child has overheard about a court case a family member is involved in or it might involve a sticky family situation (such as a divorce or family dispute) about which a child has enormous emotion but little information or understanding.

Let children know that they can tell you, their teacher, this kind of news, but not the whole class. Making this distinction not only protects the child and the family but also protects the rest of the class from access to information that is beyond their capacity to cope with or understand.

Reassure children that sometimes it's hard to decide whether certain news is suitable for group sharing. If they ever have something which feels like it could be private family news, they should always "try out" their sharing with you first to help make this judgment.

Getting Started

Prepare students to handle the sharing of serious news.

Community news can be light, humorous, or matter-of-fact. It may also be sad and painful or worrisome. When the classroom climate is safe and comfortable, both kinds of news can be offered and received with care and respect.

Younger children tend to blurt out what they need to say when they need to say it. With the help of their teacher, however, they are very able to recognize that some news is serious and demands a different kind of response than other, lighter news. As teachers, we can model a response: "I'm sorry to hear that your dad is in the hospital."

Older children can be more deliberate about the sharing of serious news. Some teachers of older children introduce labels for the two types of community news—newsy news and serious news, for example. When a class first begins using the format of Sharing, most news offered naturally tends to be newsy news. When class members are at ease with the structures of sharing, questions, and comments, and when they trust each other to respond easily and respectfully to newsy news, you might inform the group that they are ready to add serious news.

Emphasize that the children should always bring serious news to you first and you will determine whether it's appropriate to share with the group. In some cases, you may need to help a child modify the serious news in order to make it appropriate; in other cases, you may need to explain to a child that the news is not suitable to share with the class. Let parents know ahead of time that you will

*Sharing offers opportunities for children to develop
a repertoire of responses to different kinds of news.*

Sharing

be introducing serious news and that you will be carefully filtering any serious news the children bring for Sharing.

Through discussion and brainstorming, help the children sort and categorize their news. What are some examples of newsy news? Serious news? It is also helpful to generate ideas for constructive responses to different kinds of news. If someone shares something sad, what can we say to let them know that we listened well and that we care how they feel?

These are not skills commonly taught. Recently, I saw a book titled *How to Say It,* offering "ready-to-use letters to suit every personal or professional occasion no matter what the situation." The market for such books indicates that, even as well-intentioned adults, we struggle to know what the "right" words are. Too often, our awkwardness and discomfort can cause us to avoid acknowledging another's pain or offering our help. The practice provided by responding to news in Sharing can help us feel more competent at navigating these situations.

Sharing responsibilities

In implementing and assessing Sharing, keep the following general responsibilities in mind.

Teachers' responsibilities

- Set up systems for signing up and for the number of questions and comments allowed
- Act as facilitator and timekeeper, keeping the process moving
- Model good oral communication skills
- Model appropriate language for questions and comments
- Help students keep the focus upon the sharer
- Screen out sharing that is inappropriate for the group

Students' responsibilities

- Choose news that is appropriate to share with the group
- Organize their ideas and keep their sharing brief
- Wait their turn to share
- Place any objects they need in the designated Sharing place
- Listen attentively to others' sharing
- Ask questions and make comments that show interest, respect, and caring
- Stay focused upon the sharer

Getting Started

Fine Tunings

FINE TUNINGS

Q. *What should I do when a child starts telling about something that's really inappropriate for Sharing time?*

A. Sometimes children are honestly not sure what category some news falls into and may begin sharing a piece of news that feels inappropriate to you.

Perhaps it is a piece of family news that isn't for public consumption, or perhaps it is news that is too scary for the class to handle. Occasionally, children manipulate attention by using shocking or disturbing revelations.

The mother of seven-year-old Katie is a reporter and is privy to many details of a particularly gory local murder. Though you know that she tries to protect Katie from hearing more than she needs to, Katie's powers of hearing and over-hearing are highly developed and she specializes in eavesdropping on phone calls and conversations that are saved for after her bedtime.

"There's a lot of stuff about the body of that guy," she begins her sharing one day, "stuff that the police aren't telling people." Your "Appropriateness Detector" is beeping loudly. Intervene without overreacting and move on. "Katie, I'd like you to hold onto the rest of your sharing until I can talk with you about it later. I'm not sure that it is news for our whole class to hear."

Listen to Katie as soon as possible after Meeting ends and let her know whether her news is suitable for the classroom audience or should be saved for you. In a case such as this one, a phone call to the parent is also in order.

Q. *What should I do when students don't speak loudly enough for others to hear them? Or when they can't understand a particular child? Should I repeat that child's words?*

A. Though this is a situation calling for individual judgment, a general guideline is to resist "voice-overs." Allow sharers to speak for themselves unless there are severe speech problems or some other issue clearly creating communication difficulties. Make sure students know and use courteous ways of telling a child that they didn't hear or understand something that was said. This is important feedback for speakers, and it is necessary for the conversation to continue.

Q. *Is it all right for me to ask questions and make comments or should I leave that to the other students?*

A. It is definitely all right for you to ask questions and offer comments. In fact, it is vital for students to see that you find their news interesting and that you care about how things are going for them. It's also a good opportunity to model questions and comments in an unobtrusive way.

However, it's best to allow students to respond first and be sure not to respond to every single sharing. If you do, the message is that an exchange isn't really valid until the teacher has spoken.

Having a designated shelf for any objects brought in
for Sharing can alleviate many problems.

Fine Tunings

Q. *I know I should discourage responses that involve the responder's experiences rather than focusing on the sharer—comments like "I have a dog, too, and..." But sometimes it seems like those responses are honest attempts at connection and empathy, not simple egocentrism. Is it ever OK to allow such comments?*

A. This questions involves an important distinction, a judgment call we must make as we guide Sharing. Is the intention of the response to highlight a connection with the sharer and acknowledge a bond revealed by the sharing? Or is the intention to divert the focus from the sharer to the responder and his or her news?

Like many distinctions, this is not always clear and tidy. What begins as an acknowledgment of connection can unintentionally slide quickly into one's own sharing. When that happens, the teacher needs to stop the commenting child with a respectful reminder, "That sounds like some interesting sharing about you, Chris. You could share it tomorrow when it is your turn. Now you can ask Bruce a question or make a comment about his sharing."

The goal is to help children respond to another's experience without bringing it back to themselves. Some teachers give students a specific phrase to help them frame this kind of response, a phrase which lets them draw upon their own genuine connections while remembering their job of keeping the focus on the sharer. "I have a connection to you, Chris, because we have a car like that. Maybe we can talk about it later."

Q. *I often run into problems with the logistics of children bringing in objects to share. Children can't find the object when it's their turn to share. Everyone in the circle wants a chance to touch the object. Arguments occur over how classmates handle the object. With so much attention focused on the object itself, how can I keep the child's sharing from getting lost in the shuffle?*

A. The sharing of objects can create lots of problems in addition to the "Bring and Brag" syndrome previously discussed. There are a variety of strategies you may want to use if you are going to have children bring in objects for Sharing. One is to designate a "Show Shelf" or "Sharing Basket" in your room. When children bring in an object for Sharing, they leave it in this spot where others are able to view it but not touch it.

Once the object is shared, it's put back on the shelf until the end of the day. If the sharer wants children to handle the object later in the day, the sharer can explain and demonstrate during Sharing how the object should be handled. Finally, as a general rule, don't allow objects to be passed around the circle. It usually takes a very long time during which the focus is shifted from the sharer to the object itself.

Sharing

Q. *There are lots of questions in response to sharings in my classroom, but seldom any comments. Why is that and what can I do?*

A. The situation you name is quite common in classrooms. Chip Wood, author and teacher of both children and adults, sees a difference between questions and comments that helps explain it. He notes that question-asking is essentially egocentric; questions usually arise from information that you wish for yourself. Commenting, by contrast, requires empathy, the ability to take another's perspective and think about what he or she needs in order to feel cared for at that moment. Finding language to empathize can be challenging and may feel risky.

It's important to help your class understand the difference between questions and comments and to provide low-risk opportunities to practice making comments. Try offering news of your own as material upon which to practice: "This morning I am going to share about something that happened to me on the way to school and I want only comments—not questions, but comments—from the audience. On the way in to school today I dropped all my papers in a puddle in our parking lot. I'm ready for comments."

Choose a common situation with which all students can identify. We need to learn to respond to the everyday pleasures and irritations as well as the moments of high drama which comprise our lives. With practice, we can build our vocabulary for caregiving and we can achieve a comfort level that lets us use it.

Group Activity

BUILDING WHOLE-CLASS IDENTITY

"Let's recite our class poem," announces the teacher and nineteen seven- and eight-year-old voices dutifully offer up a sing-song rendition of the October stanza from Maurice Sendak's poem "Chicken Soup with Rice." (Sendak 1962)

In October
I'll be host
to witches, goblins
and a ghost.
I'll serve them
chicken soup
on toast.
Whoopy once
whoopy twice
whoopy chicken soup
with rice.

"We've got the words down," says their teacher, "and now we're going to do it in our scary voices. Take a minute and think about how you can make your voice sound scary."

Eyes twinkle and smiles flicker on their faces as the second graders ponder and await their teacher's signal to begin. In a dramatic transformation from their earlier version, the young voices have grown deep and slow and mysterious. As they finish, the smiles that had flickered earlier erupt into full-fledged grins and chuckles. They revel in the sound of their collective voice.

"Mmmm…very nice. Let's think about reciting that at next week's All-School Meeting," compliments their teacher.

Down the hall the first graders are singing the Friends' Song. "Friends, friends, one, two, three. All my friends are here with me. You're my friend…" They already know it in English, Spanish, and French. Today they will learn how to perform it in sign language.

On the second floor, the fifth graders are intent on guessing a category made up by their classmate, Caleb, who is doling out indirect clues in a game called Aunt Minerva *(Appendix F)*.

"Aunt Minerva likes Florida but doesn't like Alaska," announces Caleb.

No responses.

Introduction

Caleb tries again. "Aunt Minerva likes heavy down quilts but doesn't like thin sheets."

Two hands shoot up and Caleb calls on Sonya.

"Aunt Minerva likes soup but doesn't like ice cream?" ventures Sonya, her voice making the statement a question.

Group activities are short and fast-paced,
and involve everyone in the class.

"That's true," nods Caleb.

"Danny?" Danny has retracted his hand after hearing Sonya's contribution. "Nope, I'm not ready yet."

After a few more guesses about Aunt Minerva's preferences, half the hands in the circle are raised, and Mr. Bergstrom, the teacher, spots a good stopping place. All have grappled with the process of set-making but the "who-hasn't-got-it-yet" syndrome hasn't set in.

"Pick a guesser, Caleb," Mr. Bergstrom directs, and Caleb points to Josie.

"Is it hot and cold?" she asks.

Caleb's smile and nod confirms it.

PURPOSES AND REFLECTIONS

As the above vignettes illustrate, group activities are short, fast-paced activities involving everyone in the class. Some activities have clear academic skill-building components and may tie in to current topics in the curriculum; other activities appear "just for fun" and offer practice in more generalized skills like listening, following directions, exercising self-control, or rolling the ball gently.

Purposes of Group Activity

- **Contributes to the sense of community culture by building a class repertoire of common material—songs, games, chants, and poems**

- **Fosters active and engaged participation**

- **Heightens the class's sense of group identity**

- **Encourages cooperation and inclusion**

Group Activity contributes to the sense of community culture by building a class repertoire of common material— songs, games, chants, and poems.

It's clean-up time and Shawna and Leo are methodically taking the large wooden unit blocks from their skyscraper and stacking them neatly on the appointed shelf. "Whoopy once, whoopy twice," chants Leo under his breath as he leans from the pile of blocks to the shelf, lost in his rhythm of stack and tidy and lean again. Shawna, done with the dismantling of their creation, moves closer to help him. "Whoopy chicken soup with rice," she chimes in. Her voice layers over her companion's as neatly as the blocks they stack on the shelf.

The chants and songs, games and story lines that are introduced during Group Activity time are a common and crucial currency in the classroom community. They contribute to a shared archive from which children can draw when they are riding the bus together on a field trip, in a companionable clean-up moment, or at the snack table. We feel a sense of belonging, comfort, and acceptance when we recognize a familiar melody, when we are invited into a game and realize that we know the rules, when someone refers to a funny story and we find that we know that story, too. We are at home in this place, with these people.

Purposes and Reflections

Sometimes the common learning provides us with a way to affirm our group identity within a larger community. When the second grade stands before the rest of the school and intones their ghosts and goblins stanza of "Chicken Soup," it is a wonderful declaration of their solidarity. As they stand together and speak with one voice to the audience, they are clearly a cohesive group.

Group Activity fosters active and engaged participation.

Good choices for group activities are active rather than passive and require everyone's participation. They can be a great "wake-up call" at the outset of the day because they demand that each of us pay attention and contribute. It's not easy to snooze through a fast-paced game of Ra-de-o or Zoom *(Appendix F)* or to let your attention wander when it will be your turn soon to think up an equation for today's date and the first six people have used up the obvious number statements.

Joining in the tempo of the group activity can help students find a productive pace for moving into the rest of the day. We all have different rhythms and gaits, and our differences bring richness to the group of which we are a part. But we also have our days when something in our pace is "off." We may arrive at school distracted, replaying a conflict at the breakfast table in our head. We may arrive speedy and frazzled, moving at top speed to compensate for oversleeping, needing help to change gears and settle down. Joining a group activity, moving in unison, can sometimes help us find our most comfortable stride.

For today's group activity, these children learn hand games they will later use when there is "waiting time" in the classroom.

Group Activity heightens a class's sense of group identity.

Being part of a whole group activity builds cohesiveness and deepens individuals' sense of responsibility as group members.

In *Promoting Social and Emotional Learning,* an anecdote describes how an "exemplary" high school teacher uses games as warm-up activities. One day the game was group juggling—each student receiving a ball from a specific person and tossing it to another specific person. As the game progressed and more balls were added, concentration increased and laughter erupted frequently. When discussing the game afterwards, students mentioned that having a group goal led to a sense of responsibility—everyone had to be fully alert to achieve the group goal. The laughter added to the sense of closeness among students. (Elias et al. 1997, 54)

The universal human need to have fun was discussed in the chapter, *"Morning Meeting: An Overview."* Group activities—whether they involve seeing how fast a hand squeeze can travel all around the circle or how many words can be formed from the word "December"—are often fun. They evoke smiles and laughter and a sense of satisfaction. They are also productive and teach skills useful in academic learning.

This doesn't necessarily mean that group activities are always games or activities we usually think of as "fun." The activities must demand that the group pull together and that all members are involved, but they might be a class recitation of a poem or a choral reading, daily math rituals, or group story writing.

Group Activity encourages cooperation and inclusion.

Purposes and Reflections

Good group activities allow all members to take part. Although some students will excel in certain activities, some in others, each group activity must be accessible to all. A teacher's knowledge of her class will guide the choice of activities. They shouldn't all feel easy—a sure route to complaints of "boring." But neither should activities be ones in which only a couple of "gifted" students can feel successful, for this will be demoralizing and isolating for others in the group. Celebrating individual talents and achievements is definitely healthy in a classroom, but Group Activity is not the place for it.

Successful activities often stretch and challenge the group. They work well when those stretches and challenges are deliberate choices on the teacher's part and are introduced when the group is ready to take on a challenge that will feel safe for the group and the individuals. Helping the class to notice their increasing proficiency with a challenging activity affirms the role of practice and effort in learning.

I once heard a group of fifth graders groan, "We'll never be able to say this," upon a first read-through of *The Gettysburg Address*. "We can't even pronounce half these words." And they were right. They couldn't pronounce them. Yet two weeks later, after intensive coaching and many practice sessions, these fifth graders could do more than pronounce. They proclaimed—with resonant voices and nary a stumble.

"Remember how two weeks ago you were never going to be able to recite this?" reminded their teacher. This was such an important lesson: that what seems insurmountable at first can indeed be surmounted with effort and support. Learning this lesson will serve these students well as they go on to confront the mysterious equations algebra offers, the unfamiliar constructions of a Shakespearean line, or the booklet of directions for installing the garage door opener.

Although group activities should be cooperative, not competitive, in nature, it is sometimes fun for the group to "compete" against itself. Can they beat their previous time at Telegraph, a game in which they must work together to pass a hand squeeze around the circle as quickly as possible? Can they come up with more equations for twenty-three on the 23rd of this month than they could on the 23rd of last month? Many classes enjoy keeping a log of their best times for various activities. But this kind of competition is best used sparingly, so that the emphasis remains on the activity rather than the contest.

Highlights of Group Activity

- **Provides a way for all class members to learn a common set of songs, chants, games, poems, etc.**

- **Lets the group experience working together to produce an outcome impossible as individuals or a small group**

- **Demands cooperation**

- **Encourages inclusion**

- **Fosters active and engaged participation**

- **Allows students to see each others' differing strengths**

- **Provides experience in having fun together as a group**

- **Gives an opportunity to reinforce and extend social and academic skills**

- **Allows for the integration and practice of curriculum content**

Group Activity

You may want to browse through *Appendix F* before continuing. It lists a wide variety of group activities, some of which are referred to by name in the text.

GETTING STARTED

Introduce Group Activity, modeling appropriate behaviors.

Explain that this is a time within Morning Meeting when the whole group will do an activity together. In whatever language is appropriate and respectful to the age group, note that it will be important in these activities for each person to take good care of herself or himself, as well as taking care of other people in the group.

Choosing a couple of aspects which are important to the activity for the day, model constructive behaviors related to those aspects. Eventually, you will find it helpful to model the following:

- Voice level
- Physical controls
- Taking turns
- Making mistakes
- Problem-solving

Getting Started

- Cooperative play

"Eventually" is a key word here. Opportunities to model and discuss how activities are going will happen throughout the year. Carefully choose relatively fail-safe activities at the outset so that the group experiences success without the need for extensive preparation. It is better to model one element at a time, specifically and thoroughly, than to try to conduct an exhaustive (and exhausting!) Grand Tour of constructive activity behaviors.

"Today we are going to play a fast and in-control game of Speed Ball," Mr. Coughlin tells his first grade class. "I'm going to throw the ball to Willy. Watch me and tell me what makes it both fast and in-control." He throws it low and carefully and Willy catches it easily.

"What did you notice?"

"You didn't throw it over his head," volunteers Zeke.

"That's right. And where did I aim it?"

"At his belly." Mr. Coughlin nods.

"You threw it kind of easy," offers Claire.

"Why did I do that? Wouldn't it be faster to throw it hard?"

"No," maintains Claire. "Because Willy's not that far away from you and it would probably just bounce offa' him then, or go out of the circle and he would have to go get it and then it would really slow things down."

Aaron's hand is up. It's clear, even at six, that he is a versatile and talented athlete and loves any chance to throw a ball—or talk about it! "If you were throwing at Amy or somebody all the way across the circle, you'd have to throw harder, though."

"So you noticed," summarizes Mr. Coughlin, naming specific behaviors with key words that can be quick reminders later, "that I used careful aim and a just-hard-enough throw."

"I'm going to throw it again and this time I want you to watch Willy and notice what he does that makes the catching part fast and in-control." After the class has noted that Willy keeps his eyes on Mr. Coughlin and his hands ready in his lap, the game begins. The modeling took only a few minutes and the chance for application was offered right away, important timing for these six-year-olds.

Model social as well as physical behaviors.

Some modeling addresses social rather than physical controls. Mr. Roth is determined that his fourth grade classroom will be one in which it is fine to make a mistake. It is a message he conveys day-in and day-out in a number of ways, from the poster on the wall that says "The only person who doesn't make a mistake is a person who never does anything" to the stories culled from his own everyday life which often include an error in thinking and the learning he gained from it. It is not a message accepted easily by his nine-year-old students who are painfully aware and critical of their own and their peers' imperfections.

Group Activity

"When we do an activity like Number Equations, we will sometimes make mistakes. I want us to be able to notice mistakes in a way that is honest and respectful so that we can learn from them. Today is the 4th. Jocelyn (an able math student), please make up an equation for the 4th that has a mistake in it. I'm going to be a student who catches the mistake. Watch me and notice how I respond."

"One hundred divided by twenty is four," offers Jocelyn, writing it on the chart.

Mr. Roth looks thoughtful for a moment and then slowly puts his hand up. Hamming it up just a bit, he switches chairs, mimes calling upon himself, moves back to his student chair and says, "I think that one hundred divided by twenty is five."

"What did you notice?"

"You didn't shoot your hand up really fast, like: 'Ooh, ooh, I see a mistake!'" Kelly mimes an over-eager response.

"You kept your voice nice and didn't sound know-it-all."

"You didn't laugh or roll your eyes."

"You said what you thought was right, not that Jocelyn was wrong."

Mr. Roth reframes in positive terms. "So honest and respectful mistake-noticing means that we stop and think first, and use a polite voice and body language when we suggest someone made a mistake."

"Yeah, 'cause it could be you the next time!" blurts Hank. Smiles of recognition reply.

Mr. Roth is pleased that his students recognize the helpful and not-so-helpful details. He also knows that habits don't change easily and that eyes will roll and hands will wave excitedly at a mistake, perhaps not today with this lesson fresh in their minds, but tomorrow or surely next week. And he will remind, redirect, and reinforce—always respectfully, as he has asked them to do when they notice others' mistakes.

Choose activities that fit the group at this particular time.

Choosing activities highlights the teacher's role as balance-keeper and as knower-of-the-group. The season of the school year, the group's degree of cohesiveness and its temperament are all factors in determining which activities will be most beneficial.

Getting Started

Is it the beginning of the year, before the children even know each others' names? Naming, introduction, or interview games are good. Is this a group of serious scholars who could use some lightening up? Perhaps Zoom or, with older students, Ra-De-O. Have the last three mornings of antics at Meeting and messy transitions let you know that this group needs tight structure and focus at every turn? Or maybe you have a group with a very low sense of academic self-esteem. Memorizing a serious and beautiful poem together will help them look at themselves differently.

There are many categories of activities with a number of modifications and variations that will help meet the day-to-day needs of every group:

- Physical/high energy activities
- Silly/fun activities
- Intellectual games/puzzle activities
- Creative/artistic activities

Use your observations and knowledge of your ever-growing group as you design a menu of different activities for and with your class. *Appendix F* offers a wide variety of group activities to help you get started.

Group Activity responsibilities

In implementing and assessing Group Activity, keep the following general responsibilities in mind.

Teachers' responsibilities

- Choose a variety of activities which are age-appropriate and include all skill levels

- Make sure many different kinds of activities are represented—physical, intellectual, artistic

- Give directions that are simple, clear, and consistent

- Make sure everyone knows the rules of activities

- Select activities that are non-competitive

- Model being playful or enthusiastic without being silly

- Stop the activity and regroup if it's not going well

Group Activity

Students' responsibilities

- Participate fully in all activities

- Interact with all classmates

- Show respect and support for the efforts of all participants

- Have fun without being silly

- Work hard without being competitive

- Follow the rules of activities

FINE TUNINGS

Q. *I know that activities should be fun, but my class gets really silly and doesn't take them seriously. Any suggestions?*

A. You are right to draw a distinction between silliness and playfulness. While play can enhance learning, silliness is distracting and gets in the way of group engagement. Monitoring the tone is an important teacher job in Morning Meeting. Don't be afraid to stop an activity if it feels too silly or unfriendly and reminders and redirections have not helped

The next step is to do some observation or reflection. Is the silliness coming from a couple of students or is it widespread? If it comes from one or two students, consider whether there is something about the particular activity that makes it hard for them to join wholeheartedly. You may need to speak to them individually to say what you notice and ask them to think of ways they can help Group Activity work better.

If the troubling attitude is group-wide, it's time to look at the activities themselves. Perhaps it's time for very structured activities that offer challenge, that help the group take itself more seriously. Remember that it is Group Activity, not Group Game.

If varying the type of activity doesn't help, sharing what you notice with your students and inviting their thoughts about what's happening may solve the problem.

Q. *The same students seem to "star" in Group Activity. How can I address this?*

A. We must make sure that the variety of activities we present call upon many different modalities. Though it is important that everyone be able to participate in all the activities, it is true that—except for a few extraordinarily well-rounded individuals—we all have different areas where we shine and areas where we struggle. Group activities allow us to see ourselves and each other, teachers included, in those shinings and those struggles.

Some of us are graceful and coordinated; some are verbally quick and playful. Some have terrific recall and excel at memory games and recitation; others are theatrical and can pantomime any emotion down to its every nuance. Still others have a gift of melody that enables a class to sound beautiful when they sing together.

Group Activities can spring from the daily curriculum;
here, the teacher leads the students in a spelling activity.

Making sure our activities engage many different aptitudes ensures that all children will have experience in the role of leader and in the role of "leaner." All will get to feel foolish and all will get to feel smart. Robby learns that when he stands next to Casey he can, in fact, carry a tune. Meg learns that if she forgets a line in the skit, she can glance at Noah who will remember and give her a cue.

As the group comes to know and rely upon each other, a group intelligence develops that enables some brilliant moments of ensemble play, times when the class pulls off something together that is clearly more than the sum of their individual efforts.

Corporations pay big dollars these days to experts who present seminars and teach employees the skills of team-playing and attempt to build group intelligence. It is the way workers must learn to work, say futurists. Schoolchildren engaged in a group activity practice it every day.

Q. *There is a boy in my class who hangs back and never participates in Group Activity. How can I encourage him to join?*

A. This is a situation in which a teacher's knowledge of her individual students is crucial. What does this boy choose to do at recess or choice times?

What are his areas of comfort and skill? If it is Gerry, who excels at anything with the suffix "-ball," I would choose something involving ball-throwing. If it is Casey, who has a wealth of information about the latest world conflict or most recent movie blockbuster, then I would structure an activity around current events. If the activity is a new one for your group, you might elicit this student's help ahead of time to try it out and co-teach it to the group with you.

Q. *I've run out of ideas for group activities and it's starting to feel like one more thing I have to make "fun." I'm feeling burdened by it and my students don't seem to be having much fun with it either. Am I just not creative enough?*

Fine Tunings

A. It's true that in Group Activity, as in almost everything in our classrooms, the teacher's sense of engagement and pleasure is contagious. And the reverse is true. If you are consistently feeling uninspired and weighed down by a certain part of the routine, your class will perceive it.

Sometimes we work too hard to make things "fun." Play and engagement are as much about a way of doing something as they are about the content of what we are doing. Remind yourself that although the best learning is highly entertaining, it is not your role as a teacher to be an entertainer. Group activities needn't be one more thing; they can spring from the program you are already working hard to plan for your students.

Picture these scenes. A group of seventh graders, totally involved, mentally wrestle together with a tricky logic problem. Down the hall, the third graders are clapping out the syllables in their weekly list of spelling words, feet tapping along. In the primary room, the kindergarten and first grade class are proudly "reading" in unison a poem hand-lettered in large clear print on the easel in the circle. In another primary class, students are using their bodies to make a beaver lodge and act out the activities of a beaver colony, representing and extending the learning they have gained from their study of beavers who inhabit a nearby pond.

All of these activities come straight from the curriculum in the room. They are not imported just for activity time and they are not games. They meet the criteria for Group Activity perfectly: they are noncompetitive and inclusive; they require attention and alertness; they build the group's sense of how they can problem-solve together; they develop a group voice, intelligence, and identity.

Finally, consider shifting some of the responsibility for making the activities work from you to your students. Many teachers, after introducing a new activity, ask the group two reflective questions:

1. What made it work?

2. What made it fun?

This gets the children thinking about how they work together and leads to an increase in their investment.

**Group
Activity**

Morning Message

A LETTER TO THE CLASS

The group activity finished, Ms. Adams turns to the chart on an easel next to her, physically adjusting it a bit so that it is visible to all in the circle. Her third graders take this moment to adjust themselves, too, settling themselves for the Morning Message part of Morning Meeting. The message on the chart involves some questions about months of the year and days of the month, a current topic in the class's math program. (See chart on the following page.)

Ms. Adams points to the blanks provided for the date. "No one filled in the date yet. Who can tell me the date today?" Almost every hand goes up.

"Let's hear how some people figured out what day of the month it is."

"I looked at the calendar and I knew that today is the last Monday of the month. And I read what month it is at the top of the calendar page. But I remembered that anyway."

"I used tally marks from our calendar countdown on the chalk board."

Ms. Adams hands a fat green marker to a child whose hand is up. "Alyssa, fill in the date, please."

Morning Message continues with a student selected to read the message, followed by a discussion about months of the year based on what students have filled in at the bottom of the chart. Together, students check the accuracy of their filled-in answers and complete the remaining one. Their teacher points out that months always begin with upper case letters and gives a mini-lesson on articulation when she notices that most of the class isn't saying the "th" sound at the end of the ordinal numbers on the chart.

Pointing to the last sentence on the chart, the teacher reads it again. "What do I mean by 'productive'? Let's think of some synonyms." Hands go up and ideas are ventured.

"Great"

"Terrific."

"Smart."

"Enjoyful."

Ms. Adams acknowledges each adjective with a nod, commenting after the last, "Yes, we do feel good when we're productive. We enjoy it. You are giving me great synonyms for a word like 'fantastic.' Can you think of a word or a couple of words that means almost the exact same thing as productive?"

There is a long pause before Tyler's hand goes up. "A working hard day."

"Yes, that defines it well!"

Introduction   Ms. Adams glances at her watch. "I have just a couple of announcements about today. This morning those who didn't bake yesterday will be baking corn bread

For more examples of Morning Message
charts, go to Appendix H.

Hello, Great Thinkers!

Today is _____ ___, ___.

Today _Sharla_ will lead our Greeting. _Charlie_ and _Tate_ will share. We will recite our October poem.

This month is ending. How many days are left? _5_ How many days have passed? _25_ What month follows October? _November_

What month is the _____th month of the year?

1st _january_
7th
10th _October_
5th _May_

Have a super productive day.

with Rafe's mother. Other than that we will have a regular Tuesday. You've paid attention through a long meeting. Now let's stand." They push their chairs back, anticipating what's to come. "Stretch up, get the kinks out, now hug yourselves tight, heads up, now down to your knees. Let's come up slowly…"

PURPOSES AND REFLECTIONS

Morning Message provides information and group academic work through a message written by the teacher on a chart each day. While the contents and format of the message change as children get older, as well as the way it is read before and during Meeting, the methods and purposes stay the same.

Before Meeting begins, children read the message as they enter the room and follow any instructions on it. The chart is then moved into the Meeting circle and used as the basis for the last component of Meeting each day. During that time, the message on the chart is read, then discussed with quick activities based on the chart.

Morning Message

Purposes of Morning Message

- **Eases the transition into the classroom day and makes children feel excited about what they'll be learning**

- **Develops and reinforces language, math, and other skills in a meaningful and interactive way**

- **Builds community through shared written information**

You may want to browse through *Appendix H* to familiarize yourself with some sample Morning Message charts before continuing. You can use them for reference in the sections that follow.

Morning Message eases the transition into the classroom day and makes children feel excited about what they'll be learning.

Seeing an attractive and interesting chart waiting at the beginning of the day is one way of letting children know that their teacher is ready for them, has thought about the day, and is welcoming them to it. It supplements face-to-face greetings and "check-ins" rather than replacing them.

**Purposes
and
Reflections**

The chart invites children to participate even before Meeting begins.

Information on the chart acclimates students to the day and allows them to reflect on learning and events of previous days. The chart often invites them to begin participating even before Meeting: "Draw a food that you saw on our trip to the store yesterday." "Can you find a spelling mistake or two in this message?" "List one fact you know about Sojourner Truth."

Included on the chart is a message from the teacher, telling the children about something they will be learning that day. The teacher may highlight one thing from all of the content that will be taught that day, which will make the children feel excited about what's ahead. This message can also include notes about "specialists," announcements about anything happening that is out of the ordinary (visitors, assemblies, field trips, etc.), and what will happen directly after the close of Meeting. In this way, Morning Message helps prepare children not only for the beginning of the school day and Meeting but also for the shift from Meeting to the rest of the classroom day.

Morning Message develops and reinforces language, math, and other skills in a meaningful and interactive way.

For younger children, who are learning to read and write, the daily use of the written chart teaches reading, language arts, and math skills through meaningful information and relevant questions. The language patterns used on the chart are deliberately predictable and repetitious from day to day. They include familiar sight vocabulary and reflect content from classroom life.

"Freddy is first. Maura is the door holder. Today is…" These simple sentence patterns, to which even the youngest quickly become accustomed, teach letter and number recognition, phonic skills, word families, and spelling and language patterns.

Including one or two sentences at the end of the chart that are not predictable or repetitious lets children develop and practice strategies for independent reading of unfamiliar language. The content of these sentences is drawn from the day's activities or curriculum. This helps motivate students, provides another opportunity to orient them to the day, and presents vocabulary that they will encounter again. "We will finger-paint." "We will talk about our spider today."

During Morning Meeting, the teacher asks questions or plays quick games based upon the information on the chart. For example:

- Who can find the letter "t"?
- Who can find two letters that go together and make the sound "ba"?
- Who can tell a number sentence for the number five?
- Who can name something in our room that we have five of?

Questions and activities can include a range of skills that offer challenges but allow success. Children need to start their day with feelings of mastery and competence. Teachers keep these questions and games fast-paced, especially when individual children are coming up to the chart to write or find something, so that the entire group is kept involved.

Before there are readers in the group, the teacher often stands at the chart in the morning, helping children read it before Morning Meeting, or the reading can be done at Morning Meeting. As children become able to read the chart on their own, teachers often pair those who are not yet readers with partners who have learned to be "reading guides." When children help each other in this way, both partners benefit and what is learned can extend far beyond the content of the chart, far beyond the acquisition of phonics skills. The following piece of writing, an excerpt from an essay my daughter wrote as part of an application to secondary school, is testimony to what is learned. In it she remembers her experience helping a classmate who had severe difficulty learning to decode words.

By fourth grade Pauline had begun waiting for me in the mornings next to the chart we were supposed to read as we came into the room. She would run her fingers over and over the words, her mouth moving slowly, trying to reach the word that would most make

Morning Message

sense. I first began to help her by standing next to her and reading aloud the message. I was filled with empathy as I began to see what a struggle the simple things I did daily were for her. A few days later I asked if she wanted help with some of the more difficult words, and within weeks we had established an understanding that she would point to the words that she did not recognize and we would sound them out together. This continued to work, and as we grew more comfortable with each other she asked me if I would help her read the message aloud, sounding out the words. From there on I can remember every morning standing by the chart and working endlessly on the same "Good morning" or "Today we will be…" I have no memory of learning to read myself, but I do clearly remember the hours I spent helping Pauline.

Purposes and Reflections

For older children, who have moved from learning to read and write to reading and writing to learn, the message will be more complex. Often teachers find that the format of a "letter to the class" works well. "Dear Friendly Workers," it might begin one day. On the Friday of a week of rain, "Dear Soggy Students" might be the salutation. The date is still included. Often the message includes an item that lets students learn about each other — "Who has a birthday this month?" "Who has the middle name 'Rose'?" or a tally, like "Sign your name here if you have a cat."

Reminders of responsibilities—"Jamie leads Sharing today"—may be listed along with news or reminders about the day: "We will have a visitor from _____" or "Bring your writing to Meeting today and be ready to share your opening sentence." Punctuation errors may be deliberately inserted for students to find and fix or math problems presented for solutions.

Even with older students, however, this is not a time for new instruction. It is a time for practicing skills and for peer learning. It is a lively, short warm-up with the goal of sending students into the day feeling engaged and capable.

Morning Message builds community through shared written information.

Responsible citizens stay informed about what's going on in their community. Morning Message is one way that we can allow students to practice that responsibility in their classrooms.

When I read my local newspaper each morning, I skim for names I know, news that affects my town, meetings I might want to attend, births, deaths, land transfers, or environmental issues I care about. I follow a similar process with the *New York Times* for national and international news. I must spot something in the headlines that piques my interest or makes me realize that this news is of

*During Meeting, the teacher uses the chart to ask questions
or play quick games that offer challenges but allow success.*

**Morning
Message**

import to me. Sometimes what catches my attention is not purely informational but engages my skills at vocabulary or logic (the puzzle pages) or simply makes me smile (comics). I pick and choose and assemble a collage of news and announcements that keeps me informed about the community in which I am a citizen.

The daily message we create for our students shares much with my daily newspaper perusing. However, we do the picking and choosing of items and assemble them for our students, using what we know about their development, their skills, their pleasures, and the programs of our classrooms. We must make the content full of pertinent information, with inviting activities—and we must expect that all will use it.

Highlights of Morning Message

- Features a written message which welcomes and greets students as they enter the room

- Gets children excited about what they'll be learning that day

- Adds predictability and structure to entering the classroom

- Contributes to students' sense of safety and being cared for by letting them know that the teacher has prepared for the day and is ready for them

- Affords a fun and interactive way to teach written language, math, and other skills

- Conveys that reading is a valuable way to get information you need

- Builds community through shared written information

- Provides a "warm-up" for the day's activities

- Eases the transition from Morning Meeting to the rest of the day

Purposes and Reflections

Getting Started

You may want to review the chart ideas in *Appendix G* and the sample charts in *Appendix H* before going on.

GETTING STARTED

Introduce Morning Message.

Let students know that every day there will be a message from you which they should read before Meeting and that it will be used at the end of Meeting as well. Model reading and reacting to the message for that day. Depending upon the age and reading level of your students, you may read to them, have them read in chorus, take turns reading, have one student read while others follow along, or have older children paraphrase what's on the chart.

Plan the logistics of the message chart.

Most teachers prefer using a chart stand and easel paper for their message, rather than the chalkboard. In most rooms, this makes the message chart easier to physically move and incorporate into the Meeting circle. Using paper and markers eliminates the risks of smudges and erasures and allows the chart to be saved and posted after Meeting time. Some teachers put old charts in the class library for children to read during language arts or send them home with individual children, such as the Student of the Day or the Line Leader.

You will need to choose a spot for the chart that is prominent and greets students as they enter the room. However, it should be a spot that will not interrupt early morning traffic flow when several children are clustered around the chart, reading or responding to the message. Keeping it in the same spot every morning helps make it part of the classroom routine.

Morning Message

Tailor content, format, and activities to your particular class.

Part of what makes a Morning Message chart of real interest is its pertinence to the classroom life of this particular group at this particular time. To be real and

The chart message on this April morning invites kindergartners to "draw something that grows."

immediate, our messages must be specific to each day and class. Although it is fine, even essential, to develop a boilerplate, if the sentences don't change and are irrelevant to the day, then they'll stop being engaging.

With younger groups in which most students are not yet fluent readers, even the predictable parts of the chart are specific to the day, including such information as today's date, the name of today's line leader, today's door holder. Additional content usually springs from current activities: "We will work with clay today" or "Look at our egg before Meeting."

With older groups, where reading skills are established, there is room for more variation in format, but the information should still derive from classroom activities and interests. Perhaps it's World Series time and excitement is high; the chart might feature a math problem involving statistics from yesterday's game. Recess didn't work well yesterday? The chart might direct students to be prepared to share at Morning Meeting one way they think they can make recess better today. If capitalization is something you note many students struggling with in their writing, the Morning Message activity could involve

Getting Started

A seventh grader points out a spelling error in the Morning Message chart, an error deliberately inserted by the teacher.

discussion of which words should be capitalized.

Using this type of content, the message becomes one more way to communicate with students about ongoing classroom affairs and subjects; it should not require separate and additional content creation.

Keep it simple.

Particularly in older grades, it can be tempting to make the chart comprehensive, squeezing in just one more thing students really ought to be thinking about, one more type of spelling mistake. This can get overwhelming, both for the students who must read and act upon the chart information and for the teacher who must create it.

Remember—the purposes of the Morning Message component are to welcome and greet students, to orient them and get them excited about their day, sometimes to accomplish an administrative task that doesn't require elaboration, and to use the written format of the chart for a quick "warm-up" skill-builder. Resist the temptation to launch into a full-blown lesson based on a spelling error students didn't catch or to list on the chart everything students will need to know about tomorrow's field trip.

Instead, file away the spelling error for a mini-lesson before writing time later this week. Perhaps next week a message chart will feature six examples of words with that spelling pattern. And if the field trip requires substantial preparation and reminders, then a separate field trip meeting in the afternoon is in order.

Morning Message, coming at the end of Morning Meeting, serves as a transition into the rest of the day. We want students to leave the Meeting feeling a sense of their competence and equipped to navigate their day. It is important, therefore, that the last few minutes of Meeting be well paced and uncluttered, not crammed with hurried instructions and partially understood communications, no matter how well-intentioned.

Also resist the temptation to post your schedule for the day on the chart. While this information is important and the schedule should be posted somewhere, the chart is not the place for it. If the chart simply contains a list of the day's activities, many children will stop reading it. Instead, the content of the chart should change daily, highlighting perhaps one thing from all the content you'll be teaching that day.

**Morning
Message**

Morning Message responsibilities

In implementing and assessing Morning Message, keep the following general responsibilities in mind.

Teachers' responsibilities

Getting Started

- Prepare the message chart before students arrive

- Model good printing or cursive writing and correct usage in the written message

- Use predictable language patterns

- Incorporate ongoing curriculum into the message and the activity

- Select the best format for reading the chart in Meeting (unison, teacher reading with students, one reader, several readers, paraphrasing)

- Choose individual students to unscramble, decode, find errors, etc., while still keeping the whole group involved

- Vary the kinds of skills featured in the chart activity

- End with announcements to help students make a transition to the rest of the day

Students' responsibilities

- Read the message upon entering the room

- Follow any directions in the message

- Read or follow along with the reading of the chart during Meeting

- Participate in activities based upon the chart before or during Meeting

- Listen to announcements presented

FINE TUNINGS

Q. *My students really like reading the message chart, but I find it hard to keep thinking of new things to write each day. I feel like it's taking me more time than it should to prepare the chart.*

A. You have lots of company, particularly among teachers of students in intermediate and upper grades. The predictable sentence starters and additional sentence or two that are just right for primary students are not challenging enough for older students.

Remember the recommendation from *Getting Started* about using the daily life of the classroom as a springboard for your message and activity. Look to your ongoing curriculum and to your general observations and knowledge of your class as sources rather than trying to think of fascinating, additional tidbits. Do your students adore riddles? Are codes really fun for them right now? Are they all really excited about the upcoming Olympics?

Some teachers have found that having a different but predictable topic for each day of the week helps them vary the content of their charts while removing the stress of total invention. Monday's chart might always feature a question or tally about weekend activities while Tuesday's chart might pose a math problem, for example. The suggestions for special topics and elements for charts in *Appendix G* illustrate many possibilities teachers have used as successful starters, which they then customize for their own Morning Meetings.

Morning Message

Q. *What's the difference between Group Activity and the Morning Message activity?*

A. Their basic purposes differ. A primary goal of Group Activity is building a sense of whole-group spirit, whereas the purpose of a Morning Message activity is to stimulate children's academic motivation and give them a chance to practice skills.

Based as they are upon the chart, Morning Message activities nearly always center upon written communication. The learning interaction often involves one student or a small, spontaneous group of students working with the material before the Meeting convenes.

There is, of course, overlap. Morning Message activities can and often do build a group's sense of itself; group activities can and often do center upon language arts or math skills. This is one of those areas requiring some attention to overall balance. If the day's group activity involves math equations, you will probably want to plan a different sort of focus for the chart activity.

Q. *I have a class with twenty-seven sixth graders and I find that there is often not enough time for doing Morning Message with an activity, particularly if our group activity has really "grabbed" the students. I can't keep students longer than thirty minutes because we team with other teachers and students for the rest of the morning's subjects.*

Fine Tunings

A. It's fine to vary the Morning Meeting format based upon your judgments about your class and what works for them. I remember a class of seventh and eighth graders I observed where a boy's sharing about a favorite old teddy bear prompted a spontaneous sort of group activity—all the members of the circle shared ways they helped themselves get to sleep at night. All the posturing which can be so prevalent at that age dropped away as, one after another, stories of beloved stuffed friends, remnants of fuzzy baby blankets, rhythmic head rocking, or foot circling emerged. When the stories were completed, only a few minutes of Meeting time remained—just enough for their teacher to make an announcement or two about the day ahead. It would have been a shame to curtail this sharing in order to fit in work with a chart or a different activity.

Some decisions about time variations happen on the spot, as in the example above. Other times, teachers know ahead of time and plan to shorten or omit certain components. Perhaps a new activity is going to be taught, or perhaps Sharing involves models of solar powered appliances that students have been building in science. A fine sense of pacing allows time for a group to fully engage while not letting things drag. Teachers should keep in mind the purposes and range of activities for each component of Morning Meeting and make sure that all are encompassed over time, not necessarily in each Meeting.

Circle of Power and Respect

MORNING MEETING IN MIDDLE SCHOOLS

BY LYNN BECHTEL

Circle of Power and Respect, or "CPR" as it's commonly called, is the middle school version of Morning Meeting. The four components of the meeting are the same as in younger grades: Greeting, Sharing, Group Activity, and Morning Message. But many of the details and emphases change to reflect the unique needs of middle school students and the structure of their school day.

CPR makes sense for middle school students. Middle schoolers, perhaps even more than younger students, thrive in the atmosphere of trust and belonging created by this ritual. Seated in a circle during CPR, all students are seen and acknowledged. They learn to greet each other with respect; communicate with power and authority without putting each other down; and listen to each other's stories, hopes, and fears. They also talk about the business of the school day ahead and learn and practice a wide range of academic skills, including language arts, math, science, geography, and test-taking.

CPR offers middle school students stability and predictability during a time in life marked by tumultuous emotional, physical, and cognitive change. And it allows students this age to do what they most want and need to do: interact with their peers. "CPR directly meets these kids' needs," says consulting teacher Anna Foot. Middle school students long to be part of the group but they're often not quite sure how to join together in a way that isn't mean and exclusive. The four components of CPR allow students to make connections with their peers in a safe, positive, and inclusive way.

In CPR, middle school children learn and practice the important social skills of cooperation, assertion, responsibility, empathy, and self-control. These skills, which form the acronym CARES, provide a needed balance to the values and social practices so prevalent in popular culture. CPR encourages cooperation rather than competition, assertion rather than aggression, responsibility rather than apathy, empathy rather than self-absorption, self-control rather than lack of control.

Developmental issues

Change is the key word to describe what happens to children between the ages of ten and fourteen. The ten-year-old who loves cooperative games, keeps his bedroom neat, and likes to hang out with his family becomes the eleven-year-old who tests limits, thrives on competition, and prefers to hang out with a select group of peers. The twelve-year-old who enthusiastically makes plans with her friends, confidently tutors younger students, and visits elders at the local nursing home becomes the thirteen-year-old who easily gets her feelings hurt, wants to work by herself on class projects, and spends hours alone in her messy bedroom. The moody and withdrawn thirteen-year-old becomes a fourteen-year-old who values relationships with peers above any adult relationship, loves to take part in group discussions, and thrives when doing service learning projects.

Accompanying these, of course, are the enormous physical changes that take place during adolescence. Familiar ten-year-old child bodies become unfamiliar and sometimes scary fourteen-year-old young adult bodies. Most girls reach their adult height at age thirteen, and boys follow a year or two later. Both boys and girls go through puberty during these years and need to contend with strong hormonal changes and the emergence of sexual feelings.

These often difficult changes are a normal part of the process of shedding child skin and emerging as an adult. Although the process can look and feel chaotic, there is a logic to it and a central question: Who am I, and who am I becoming?

In order to answer that question, children push away from family and turn towards others like themselves, their peers. In *Yardsticks: Children in the Classroom Ages 4–14,* Chip Wood says, "Adolescence is the time in which the developing person is beginning to focus on the issue of personal identity.... At fourteen 'who I am' seems to be defined by 'who we are.'" (Wood 1997, 164) In these years, acceptance by peers is of paramount importance.

Introduction to CPR

*C is for Circle, P for Power, and R for Respect.
That's what I'm talking about.
When you sit in that circle, what do you feel?
Do you feel what I feel, the power of the love and respect
everyone has for each other?*

—middle school student

In CPR, all the kids come together to form a community.

—middle school principal

*When we do CPR in the morning, we learn each other's names
and we get to know each other. We learn about what hurts [other
people's] feelings and what makes them happy. We learn how to
treat each other more respectfully. That helps throughout the day.
I see a big difference in the way [students] interact with each other
this year.*

—middle school teacher

*What is most compelling to middle school students is each other.
CPR allows them to view others and self through a safe lens.*

—middle school teacher

CPR is fun. It helps my brain relax.

—middle school student

I get to know kids. It's a good way to start the day.

—middle school student

**Circle of
Power and
Respect**

Changes in schooling

Just as the children are changing, so is the nature of their schooling. The pace and
kinds of changes vary from school to school, district to district. Some children stay
in the self-contained classrooms of elementary school through sixth grade; some

stay in their elementary school building through sixth or even eighth grade but begin to change classes and have different teachers in different subjects around grade six.

Many students, however, leave elementary school behind at age ten, eleven, or twelve and enter the world of middle school—the doorstep to high school. These children leave the self-contained classrooms of childhood—and the exalted position of oldest students in the school—and venture forth into the world of lockers, corridor chaos, homerooms, new teachers for each subject, sometimes new classmates for each subject, and bottom-of-the-heap status.

Although moving into middle school can be exciting for students—they're on their way to being grownups!—it can also be overwhelming. Block scheduling, team teaching, and student teams can make adjustment easier. Still, it's often a difficult transition that, unless carefully handled, can result in low academic achievement, serious behavior problems, and high absenteeism.

Introduction to CPR

"CPR offers another way to be"

Children between the ages of ten and fourteen are coming into the full power of their personalities and intellect. This is a critical age for learning the relationship skills and the work skills that will serve them well–or ill—in adult life. However, just when they are becoming capable of abstract, theoretical thinking—and of

Middle school students gather in the Circle of Power and Respect.

higher level moral thinking—they also become emotionally volatile, preoccupied with physical changes, and immersed in a peer culture that often says it's cool to be "bad" and uncool to be smart. All these can impede intellectual and personal growth and achievement.

More than ever in their lives, these students need a predictable routine that helps them trust each other and value learning. "CPR offers an alternative to the dog-eat-dog world that many kids live in," says Barbara Forshag, a middle school teacher from Louisiana. "CPR offers them another way to be." Beginning the day with CPR, at least three times a week, is an important step towards making school a safe and productive place for learning.

In addition, all of the components of CPR can easily be used to introduce or reinforce academic skills. Through Greeting, Sharing, Group Activity, and Morning Message, middle school students learn how to think critically, how to frame and ask good questions, how to solve problems, how to work cooperatively, and how to turn their need for peer connection into a positive and dynamic learning strategy.

Circle of Power and Respect

GREETING

It's Matt's turn to start the greeting in this eighth grade classroom. He turns to his neighbor, Kim, looks her in the eye, smiles, taps fists top and bottom, and says, "What's up, Kim?" Kim passes the greeting on to the next person, and so on around the circle.

Down the hall, a group of seventh graders are about to begin a Number Greeting (Appendix E). "What are the three things we're working on when we greet someone?" the teacher asks.

"A firm handshake," one child says.

"Eye contact," offers another.

"Saying each other's name clearly."

The teacher distributes the playing cards so that four children get the same number. She calls out "sevens," and all the children holding a seven come to the center of the room to greet one another. The greeting moves quickly as each student shakes hands and says "hello" to everyone else in the group. The students then return to their seats and the next group is called. Not only do the students have fun doing this greeting, but they get practice in standing up in front of a group, and they have a chance to connect with children they might not otherwise acknowledge.

Meanwhile, in a sixth grade classroom, students indulge in their love of riddles, puzzles, and tricks.

"Good morning, Sara," Donny says, crossing his left leg over his right.

"Good morning, Donny," Sara replies, also crossing her left leg over her right.

Sara got the trick and the greeting continues. Group members who missed the leg-crossing gesture get to watch again or "pass." A classmate, returning after a period of illness, comes in late. Students smile, wave, and whisper "Hi" as she slides into her seat. As the greeting comes to her, her neighbor leans over and gently tells her what to do: "Cross your leg and say 'Good morning,'" she softly advises. When the latecomer frowns in confusion, her neighbor says, "Just trust me." The two exchange knowing grins, and the greeting moves around the rest of the circle.

Greeting

Greeting lays a foundation for a welcoming and inclusive environment. Developmentally, middle school age children are figuring out how to form intense, loyal affiliations. One way they do this is by forming cliques or other tightly bonded and highly exclusive groups. Inevitably, there will be children who are not included in any of these groups.

So it's particularly important for this age group to learn how to welcome everyone and form groups with people other than their closest friends, and it's critical that everyone, especially the unaffiliated child, feels welcomed. Looking each other in the eye, smiling, and greeting each other by name—or a self-chosen nickname—is an important and powerful demonstration of respect that is witnessed by the entire group.

Getting Started

Pay attention to the details. They matter.

Early in the year, as children are meeting each other and learning new names, greetings should be simple—a handshake, smile, and simple "Hello" passed around the room. This is the time to model and practice appropriate facial expressions, eye contact, physical contact, and tone of voice.

Emphasize that a "Good morning" that's spoken in a mean, grudging, or sarcastic tone is not okay. Encourage firm handshakes; discourage aggressive handshakes. Help shy students to speak up. These details make an enormous difference. The skills should be modeled and practiced regularly and reinforced through ongoing debriefing sessions: "What did you notice about the way we did our greeting today?" "What makes it easier to speak loudly and clearly?"

An eighth grader greets a classmate.

Build up a repertoire of greetings.

During the first six to eight weeks of school, the teacher gradually introduces new greetings, building up a repertoire which students can draw on later in the year if they assume some responsibilities for leading CPR (see *Appendix E* for a selection of greetings).

As students become comfortable and proficient with simple "Hello" greetings, the teacher can introduce variations. One common variation is to greet one another in different languages. "We have a lot of Hmong students in our school," says one student, "So we learned to say 'Hello' in Hmong." Students can also learn greetings in Spanish, French, Urdu, Vietnamese, Farsi—or any other languages that reflect the school's population.

In another class, the students substituted a high five for a simple handshake. Variations on the Ball Toss Greeting add challenge and help build cooperation skills. The Number Greeting described earlier gives students practice in standing up in front of a group. Greetings that use songs or movements help students loosen up and laugh with each other.

Use opportunities to talk about greeting conventions.

Greeting can open discussions about how to treat each other respectfully. In a seventh grade class, for example, a student-initiated variation on the Number Greeting led to an interesting discussion about the social conventions surrounding greeting people.

Group members drew a number out of a hat to determine pairings. Then each pair met in the center of the circle and greeted one another with gestures of their choosing. However, when the first pair met in the circle, there was confusion about who should greet whom first, particularly since the teacher was one half of this pair.

The teacher explained that when he was growing up, expectations were very clear—the young deferred to their elders and used specific gestures and expressions to show respect. The students were intrigued and asked the teacher to demonstrate. A conversation evolved about formality and civility and about how words and gestures can indicate respect.

Use opportunities to practice academic skills.

Greeting

Greetings can also offer opportunities to practice academic skills. The greeting one morning in an eighth grade class was a Skip Greeting (*Appendix E*), a great one for getting students to interact with people other than their immediate neighbors in the circle.

In a Skip Greeting, the person who begins the greeting gets to choose how many places to skip. For example, the student might say, "Skip four," and then each student greets the student sitting four seats to the right. The goal is to ensure that the "hellos" will not end up where they started, but will instead flow around until everyone has been greeted. Getting this to work involves math skills. On this particular morning, Neelie announces, "Skip three."

"Take a look and think about who you will greet," the teacher says. Faces turn, some students nodding to themselves, others muttering out loud.

"I don't think this will work," Jessie says.

"It will," another asserts.

"Well, let's try," the teacher urges. "Okay, Neelie?" Neelie begins, counting herself as "one" and greets the third person in the circle, Michael. Michael counts off three and then greets the fourth person. When Neelie challenges him, he explains, "You said 'skip three.'"

"That's true," Neelie agrees. "So, what's the right way to do it?" The class finally agrees on Michael's way.

"Okay, will it work now?" the teacher asks. "Or will it end up back on Neelie?" Suddenly, a simple greeting becomes a math problem that engages the entire group.

"If the number of people in the circle is divisible by three, it won't work," suggests one student.

"If the skip number is odd and the number of us in the circle is odd…"

"If you start with yourself and then skip two….it works."

"Can we just try it?" Neelie finally asks. "I'm getting tired of thinking."

Let students share responsibility for Greeting.

As the year goes on and students become comfortable with Greeting and with each other, students can take on some of the responsibility for introducing—or even devising—the morning greeting.

Greetings that students devise can be quite creative. Consulting teacher Kathy Brady describes a "Disco Greeting" created by a seventh grader. With a '70s disco tune playing in the background, the boy who created the greeting adopted a disco dance pose as he greeted another student in the group. All the students then had to do this movement until another student introduced a new movement. For an age group that's highly self-conscious and wary of anything that might seem silly, this was a bold greeting to introduce. One important key to its success was that it was introduced well after the group had established trust with each other.

SHARING

A few weeks before the winter holidays, an eighth grade teacher begins a focused sharing about holiday gift giving. She asks students, "Do you have to give something expensive in order for the gift to be valuable? Is there anything you can give that doesn't cost anything?"

"I was so moved by their responses," the teacher said later. "A lot of these kids' families don't have much money, and the holidays really stress the students out. They came up with the most wonderful ideas! Things that they could make, things that they already had and would like to share. They suggested the gift of time, of being there to listen to someone. They really got into it and got excited about the possibilities."

In a seventh grade classroom, Graham proudly shares that he had an "awesome" visit with his mother over the weekend. The class listens intently while he describes a visit with a parent he sees only when she is sober enough. His pleasure and excitement are evident in the details he reveals. He ends his sharing with "I'm ready for questions and comments." Slowly, carefully, several hands go up. The first questions ask for more detail:

"You said your mom gave you a present. What was it?"

"What restaurant did you go to?"

"Did you have fun at the movies?"

As the students get more comfortable, their questions and comments show their understanding—and their empathy.

"Do you miss your mom a lot when she leaves?"

"I think you really like seeing your mom."

"What's your—what do you call them?—other family like?"

"What was the best part for you?"

"I met his mom," a classmate says. *"She's nice."* Graham's smile is wide and proud.

The Sharing component of CPR offers ongoing practice in respectful interaction. It enables students to explore ideas and feelings with each other in a safe way and to offer support to each other when needed.

Many sharing sessions are about the simple, but important, everyday moments in children's lives: weekend adventures, jobs, trips, extracurricular activities, athletic competitions and performances, feats and defeats. For example, in a sixth grade classroom, a girl points to a picture she's drawn of a figure sitting on a dock fishing. "I like to sit and fish," she says. "It helps me get away from things." A boy tells his class that he's moving away for a short time. "Are there any questions and comments?" he asks. "Will you be back before the end of the year?" a classmate asks him. Later, this same boy says that his favorite part of CPR is Sharing because "we all share about how we're feeling inside and how our day's going."

Sharing

Sharing gives students the skills to have "interesting, important conversations that are meaningful and inclusive," one teacher says. For instance, there was the day when Brian, a confident, mature eighth grader, led Sharing:

The teacher was surprised when Brian announced that he was going to talk about "comfort things you still have." Brian then produced a ragged blanket from his backpack. "My mom thinks I should throw this away, but I still need it to sleep at night," he told his peers, most of whom were ruled by the adolescent need to appear cool and aloof.

"Do you always bring it to school?" someone asked.

"No. Never. But I'm sleeping over at my cousin's house tonight," Brian revealed.

"What color was it originally?"

"Dark blue," Brian said. "My favorite color when I was four—I think. Does anyone else have a comfort thing?" he continued.

Brian took a big risk, but it was a risk that he felt safe taking, now that it was more than halfway through the school year and the class had built up a good deal of trust. His peers responded respectfully and affirmatively, and for the next several weeks, they eagerly shared teddy bears, blankets, dolls, and other tokens that were still loved and needed as they made their passage from childhood to adulthood.

Sharing allows students to discover the ways in which they're alike—as well as the wonderful ways in which they're diverse. Sharing allows them to pay attention to each other's experience; to practice empathy; to hear and consider divergent opinions; and to develop habits of focused thought, inquiry, and reflection that will serve them well throughout the school day and throughout their lives.

Getting Started

Take time to teach the basic format for sharing.

The basic format for sharing consists of a student making a brief statement followed by questions and comments from the group. Although this may seem simple, it's actually fairly complex. Speakers need to focus on one idea and develop that idea with relevant details. They need to speak clearly and assertively. Listeners need to sit still and pay attention. They need to formulate questions that will elicit more information and make empathic comments that extend the conversation. They need to demonstrate respect.

Many students don't have these skills and are threatened by Sharing. Consulting teacher Kathy Brady says, "Sharing is the biggest risk in the implementation of CPR for most teachers, because it involves such a risk for the students."

It's important to take the time to teach the skills necessary for sharing. Here are some guidelines:

- *Early in the year, establish ground rules about what is appropriate to share.* For example, it's okay for a student to talk about a personal achievement, interest, or worry, but it's not okay to talk about someone else or to share private family business. One teacher tells her class, "If something really bothers you, it might upset other students as well. Talk to me before you share information like this with the class."

- *Give students a format for sharing.* This will help them feel more comfortable early in the year. As they become more skilled in sharing, you can relax the structure. A common format is one sentence that states the topic and two more sentences that give details about it. Not only will students learn how to share appropriately, they'll also have a chance to practice the skills of focusing on and developing a topic—skills that they need for successful writing and public speaking.

Circle of Power and Respect

- *Model sharing, perhaps using your own experience.* "In August, my family and I took a day trip to Mt. Sunapee. We rode the chair lift to the top, hiked around, and had a picnic. Are there any questions or comments?" Using your own experience for modeling has the added benefit of letting your students begin to know you as a real person—something they greatly appreciate.

- *Take the time for students to practice sharing, talking about a topic that you assign.* They can practice with a partner or small group, or you can do a focused sharing, with each student in the CPR circle saying one thing.

Sharing

- *Follow practice with a debriefing session.* "What made this sharing easy? What made it hard? Is there anything the listener can do to make sharing easier?" Asking the question "How do you know that someone is listening to you with respect?" can stimulate a discussion about not interrupting; not being sarcastic; asking pertinent, open-ended questions; and offering reflections that are relevant to the topic.

With practice, students will learn to make empathic comments and ask probing, critical questions. "Our teacher encourages us to ask who, what, where, when, why, and how questions, which help bring up other questions," a student says. In this way, sharing helps students become critical thinkers who have the skill to differentiate between fact, opinion, and rumor.

Consider variations on the basic format.

In a variation known as a "focused sharing," everyone in the group responds briefly to a question that is generated either by the teacher or by a designated student with help from the teacher.

Carina volunteers to lead a focused sharing in a seventh and eighth grade advisory. After running the question by her teacher before CPR began, she asks the group, "What's something important that happened to you when you were little?" She pauses to give students time to think before adding, "Who wants to start?" Josh raises his hand.

"I remember riding my bike down this awesome hill and going very fast even though I wasn't supposed to. And then when I tried to brake, I skidded and...yup...broke my left arm." The class laughs along with Josh. Carina's question then goes from person to

person, each one briefly narrating an important event. Most are serious, a few are comical, all are of interest to the class. Anyone who wants to pass is free to do so.

Focused sharing is useful at the beginning of the year, when students might be hesitant to step forward. It's also a useful format for discussing "hot topics" that affect the school or local community. Again, it's important to establish ground rules about appropriate subject matter and practice how to share in a brief, respectful, focused manner. Here is a list of some possible topics for focused sharing:

- How do you feel about _____? (This could be a school, town/city, or national event affecting the students.)

- What's one accomplishment you feel proud of?

- What's one thing you like to do when you're not in school?

- If you could change one thing in the world, what would you change and why?

- If you could change one thing about school, what would you change and why?

- What person do you most admire? Why?

- Tell about a time when you showed courage.

- Tell about a time when you made a mistake.

- What's something you're looking forward to?

- If you could travel anywhere in the world, where would you go?

In a focused sharing, the responsibility of each student is to find a way to connect in a brief way to the topic. The responsibility of the group is to receive each student's comment openly and with respect. Students should always be given the opportunity to pass. Debriefing after a focused sharing can help students understand what makes some questions easy to answer, what makes some more difficult, and how the group can establish a level of trust that makes it safe to share.

Teacher sharings can be used as a springboard for lively conversation and debate.

Consider this example from an eighth grade CPR:

"I have something to share today," the teacher announces. "I was driving down to Springfield the other day and got caught in one of those traffic jams because of highway

construction," she begins. "You know, where you come to a dead stop and there's nothing you can do about it?"

She looks around the circle, noting students' nods, drawing them into her telling. "So I began to read all the bumper stickers. I realized that so many of them were nasty, negative, used curse words or made rude jokes, often about women. I started to feel angry and insulted. I wanted to tear them off the cars or make a rude comment back. Like it was personal. Do you actually notice and read bumper stickers? Is it just me?"

Hands raise. There's an immediate outpouring of bumper-sticker knowledge.

"I love reading bumper stickers," Liza states, rattling off half a dozen, many of which are funny and evoke lots of laughter. Soon everyone is sharing favorite ones. Then Frederick relates one that he saw that he thought was racist. The class gets serious again.

"Should people be allowed to have offensive things like that on their cars?" the teacher asks.

Sharing

"Well, it's your car and there's, like, freedom of speech."

"But I don't think you should be able to have mean or put-down stuff."

"You don't have to read it."

Students listen as an eighth grader shares during CPR.

"But like Mrs. C. said, it's right there in your face, and it makes you mad when you do read it." The discussion continues, filled with lively, opinionated, thoughtful contributions from the students.

GROUP ACTIVITY

The seventh graders are working intently in groups of three. They're playing Categories (Appendix F), and the first challenge is to see how many different countries the groups can name in a short period of time. After each group chooses a recorder, students spend two minutes brainstorming. At the end of the two minutes, each group counts up the number of countries listed and reports back to the class. The group with the highest number reads their list while everyone else crosses off the countries named. "Any country on your list not mentioned?" asks the teacher. Several hands wave enthusiastically. Students continue to name off countries. "Next category: rivers," announces the teacher.

Meanwhile, down the hall, a sixth grade class plays Beachball Math (Appendix F). The leader chooses to play it with factorials, something the class is working on. Most students solve their equations with relative ease; a few lean to a neighbor for help.

In yet another class, an eighth grade teacher challenges students to memorize a portion of Dr. Martin Luther King's "I Have a Dream" speech. The eighth grade students do a choral reading and talk about the meaning and significance of the speech. The teacher then asks the group, "What are some strategies we could use to memorize this speech?"

"We could read it aloud over and over again until we just know it."

"We could try to memorize one sentence at a time."

"We could have two groups and each group memorizes every other sentence."

They work on the speech all week during CPR and perform it the following week at a special all-school assembly in honor of Dr. King.

Group activities build team spirit, offer opportunities for enjoyable and active participation, encourage cooperation and inclusion, and teach social and academic skills. In the Categories activity described above, the students worked in small cooperative groups, made group decisions, spoke in front of a large group, listened to each other, and reviewed facts about geography. And they had fun in the process. In the choral reading activity, students learned about an important historical event while practicing reading, speaking, and memorization skills.

Appendix F offers a wide range of age-appropriate activities for this component of CPR. Decide what activities to introduce based on the maturity level of your class and on their experience with doing group activities. A sixth or seventh grader who is very conscious of leaving childhood behind and eager to be considered more adult, might be embarrassed by an activity that seems silly or childlike. But a fifth grader might be delighted to engage in a familiar childhood game, and an eighth grader might relish the opportunity to regress for a few minutes. The activity you do early in the year, when children are still getting to know each other and you, will be different from the activity at mid-year, when children have begun to build trust and are developing a repertoire of skills such as self-control and responsibility. And at any age, as students learn to trust each other, their resistance to "silly" activities will diminish.

Group Activity

Getting Started

Look to academics for activity ideas.

Activities don't always need to take the form of games or be physically active. Is there a logic problem that students could work through together? A word game that will build vocabulary? Could students construct a crossword puzzle that they post on a school website? Is there a poem about rivers that would make a great choral reading and tie in to the week's geography focus?

Group activity time might also be the perfect opportunity for structured, in-depth discussion. "It gives kids a chance to express opinions and learn that few things are all or nothing," says consulting teacher Anna Foot. In order for a discussion activity to work, she emphasizes, the issues need to be believable, real ones that are appropriate for the developmental span in the classroom. "Discussion can help kids bridge the gap between concrete and abstract thinking, which is a developmental step for some kids. It will open some windows—kids listen to other kids more than they do to adults."

Teach appropriate behaviors and monitor carefully.

In order for an activity to be a positive experience, you'll need to set up ground rules and teach appropriate behaviors. "Assume nothing—teach everything," middle school teacher Barbara Forshag says. It's important to agree on and consistently use a signal to get students' attention quickly. If you use activities that involve physical activity or contact, it's important to establish ground rules about how to move safely and how to touch safely.

Eighth graders have fun playing "Telegraph."

"I'll wait until everyone's listening," the seventh grade teacher announced to the noisy class before explaining the Categories activity. Later, when Chelsea was about to plunge into reading her group's list of countries in spite of several side conversations, the teacher again reminded the group of the rules, saying, "Chelsea, wait until you have everyone's attention."

Intervene when necessary.

Don't hesitate to intervene. If an activity is breaking down, stop the action immediately and redirect.

As one eighth grade class's game of Ra-de-o (Appendix F) moved slowly forward, the students who were "out" began to gather at tables around the room to talk, rather than playing their role of "static." The teacher immediately raised her hand for silence, stopping the action of the game. "You all have a role," she reminded the students. "What is it?"

"We're supposed to stand behind them and make noise so they forget what to do," a boy said.

"Right. Even if you're out, you take part in the game. Let's hear some static. Now go."

As all the students returned to the game, beeping and buzzing their static noises, the activity picked up speed and energy.

MORNING MESSAGE

"Miss, don't forget we need to read the chart," an eighth grade student reminds the teacher.

A visitor has interrupted the class's CPR and they are running short on time, but these students are intent on completing each component. The student who wrote the chart with help from the teacher goes to the front of the room. Together the students read the chart, which includes information about the day, a math challenge, and a question from the state achievement test.

Morning Message

The chart provides a focus for students when they first arrive and helps them make the transition from home to school. The chart also helps them prepare for the day. Barbara Forshag says, "If I write it on the chart, everyone knows, first thing, what's going to happen during the day. It gives students something to look forward to."

The Morning Message chart offers an additional way to build community. It offers students predictability and a concrete connection to their school community. Every day when students come to school, they can count on seeing the chart in their homeroom or advisory. The information on the chart serves to immediately engage students and offer information about the day ahead.

Typically, the chart will include a friendly salutation, announcements of classroom and school events, recognition of student achievements, commemoration of past events, and an interactive academic challenge. The academic challenge develops and reinforces language, math, and other academic skills. It also facilitates the transition into the rest of the school day.

Getting Started

Look to colleagues for ideas for academic challenges.

In addition to using ideas from your own subject area, you may want to look to other teachers for academic ideas for the chart. In one school using CPR schoolwide, teachers rotate responsibilities for coming up with an academic challenge that can be used in every classroom.

Many teachers incorporate academic challenges from their own academic discipline. A language arts teacher, for example, uses a new vocabulary word every day in the chart message. She uses the word in a sentence and then challenges the students to figure out the meaning using context clues. On the chart, students write responses to the following questions:

"What part of speech is the word?"

"What does it mean?"

"What other words mean the same thing?"

"Can you write a sentence using the word?"

During the Morning Message portion of CPR, the group then discusses the responses and clarifies any misunderstandings. A seventh grade history teacher writes the question "Do you know what today is?" and then includes historical facts about the date, followed by open-ended questions.

For more examples of Morning Message charts,
go to Appendix H.

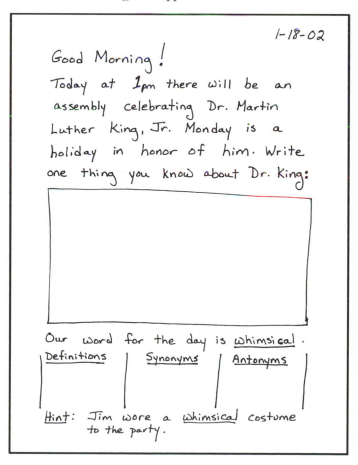

Consider this checklist when writing the chart.

However you decide to use the Morning Message chart, here's a checklist of things to consider when writing the message:

- Use a friendly, welcoming, playful tone.
- Include something that's interactive.
- Provide opportunities to practice academic skills.
- Mention individual students by name to acknowledge accomplishments.
- Refer to past group events.
- Preview the day's activities.
- Write neatly and legibly.
- Make the chart visually appealing.

General Considerations about CPR

Consider sharing responsibility with students.

Some teachers give their students some responsibility for writing the Morning Message charts, seeing this as a good way to get students more involved in running CPR.

Other teachers prefer to write the charts themselves. The advantage to this is that they then have greater flexibility in how they reinforce academic skills. For example, middle school consulting teacher Linda Crawford suggests using the chart to focus on vocabulary building. She also suggests using the interactive portion of the chart for subject-specific information. If you teach as part of a team, the team can make the charts collaboratively, focusing on math on Mondays, language arts on Tuesdays, and so forth. (See *Appendix H* for sample Morning Message charts.)

GENERAL CONSIDERATIONS ABOUT CPR

Plan to do CPR at least three times a week.

Many middle school teachers do CPR during advisory period or homeroom. Since this can be a jampacked half-hour, you might not be able to do CPR every day, but it should be part of the school day at least three times a week. Much of the benefit of CPR comes from repeated exposure to and practice of social and academic skills. If CPR is an occasional event, not only is its impact diminished, but it's also likely that the meeting itself will be less successful, since students won't have developed the skills necessary for a productive CPR meeting. As much as possible, CPR should happen on the same days so that students have a predictable structure to look forward to.

On the other days, still try to plan your advisory or homeroom activities so that they reinforce academic and social skills. For example, peer tutoring, service learning projects, team building activities, test preparation groups, career presentations, and guest speakers all offer opportunities to practice the skills learned during CPR. And these skills—respectful listening and questioning, self-control, focused presentation, cooperative learning—will help make the entire school day more successful. Another idea is to do a full CPR a few days a week and an abbreviated version on other days. For example, the class could do a full CPR three days a week and only the Greeting and the Morning Message components on the other two days.

Although it's ideal if CPR comes at the beginning of the day, it's not always possible. Some schools have advisory during second period. In that case, that's when CPR might take place. If you teach in a school that doesn't have an advisory or homeroom, you'll need to think of other options. In some cases, the principal might extend the first period from forty minutes to sixty minutes, allowing time for an abbreviated CPR. If that's not possible, you may have to look for a consistent period of time such as a sustained silent reading or study hall. Of course it's best if the whole school is working on how to incorporate CPR, with the administrators' support. If this is not the case, try to enlist the cooperation and support of team members and other colleagues.

The order of the components is important.

The order of components has a logic that makes sense for middle school children. Greeting brings students together, Sharing deepens the connection, Group Activity builds team spirit and energy, and Morning Message quiets things down and prepares students for the rest of the day. One eighth grade teacher tried switching Group Activity and Morning Message but found that her students were so revved up when they left advisory period that other teachers complained about the students' lack of focus.

Circle of Power and Respect

That said, there is some room for variation based on common sense. If it makes sense to you to vary the order or to combine two components, then try it out. Perhaps a focused sharing naturally extends into a structured discussion or a debate, eliminating the need for a separate group activity that day. The most important thing, again, is to be consistent. Having a predictable structure is reassuring to the students and ensures that you'll get to each component—and if you forget, the students will remind you!

Carefully structure opportunities for students to share responsibility for CPR.

Although you should never completely let go of the responsibility for planning and running CPR, you might wish to share with your students pieces of these tasks. When asked what he wanted teachers to know about CPR, one eighth grader said, "It's good if the kids have responsibility for it. We don't usually get to run things, but we do get to run this."

Middle school students want to have more responsibility for their lives but they're not always ready to handle the full responsibility. They need to practice, make mistakes, and learn from their mistakes under the guidance and direction of a caring adult. The various components of CPR can provide a good forum for students to practice planning and facilitation skills. But you need to prepare students well.

For the first six to eight weeks of school—longer if needed—you should be completely in charge of CPR. During this introductory period, you'll be modeling not only good group member behavior but also good group leadership behavior. You'll work with the group to set clear ground rules, to develop a repertoire of greetings and group activities, and to establish expectations for serious, thoughtful participation. This introductory period will also help you assess how well your students will handle the responsibility for planning and running CPR.

There are several models for how to share the responsibility with your students when the time comes:

Set up a work chart.

A mature group of students, particularly students who have prior experience with Morning Meeting, might set up a work chart that lists who has charge of which component on which day. You can be available as a consultant, provide a resource box or file of activities, and monitor planning and implementation.

One teacher who does this includes herself in the rotation so that she can periodically reinforce needed skills and introduce new activities. But even though this teacher shares much of the responsibility for CPR and participates in the group as a member, she never lets go of her role of adult facilitator, stopping the meeting as needed to redirect, remind, reinforce, and debrief.

Establish CPR committees.

Another model is to establish CPR committees or work groups of three or four students. Each group is responsible for planning and running an upcoming CPR. The group works together to decide on the content and duration of each component. Requiring students to present a plan to you before the meeting will allow you to have oversight of the planning process.

A variation on this is to have pairs or groups of students plan and run one component of CPR once or twice a week. These groups would need to work closely with you to ensure that the meeting is cohesive.

The most important thing to remember is that CPR should reinforce positive social skills and support academic learning. If having students plan and run the meetings interferes with this, then you'll need to reassess. Maturity and experience with Morning Meeting increase the likelihood, but do not guarantee, that students will effectively manage CPR. "The leaders in my class this year are really negative," an eighth grade teacher reported. "Even though they've done Morning Meeting for years, I have to intervene all the time to model appropriate behavior. We're taking it step by step, but it's slow."

Following are some questions to help you assess student leadership of CPR. Based on the answers to the questions, you might adjust the level of responsibility you give students.

- Are student leaders helping the group interact in a positive, inclusive way, or are interactions often negative and sarcastic?

- Are student leaders helping the class move to a deeper level of communication, or are they simply going through the surface motions?

- Are students adhering to the ground rules and living up to the expectations that were established at the beginning of the year, or are they getting lax?

- Are meetings continuing to feel fresh and lively, or are they stale, with the same old activities and greetings repeated many times?

- Are students including activities that challenge the mind and support academic learning, or is there a disproportionate emphasis on play?

It's also important to pay attention to your personal style. If you're more comfortable maintaining control of planning and leading CPR throughout the year, do so. One seventh grade teacher plans and runs every meeting, knowing that she's giving the students a good foundation for taking on the responsibility of leading some portions of CPR when they move on to eighth grade. Anna Foot expresses concern that students might go through the motions correctly but wouldn't understand why each component was important. "It may appear right because they get the 'how-to'," she says. "But without the 'why' the meeting has no purpose." But even if you retain control of planning and leading the meeting, remember that it is a good learning opportunity for the students if they sometimes get to lead an activity or greeting or write a Morning Message chart.

General Considerations about CPR

FINE TUNINGS

Fine Tunings

Q. *Why do you call this CPR? My students know what Morning Meeting is. Can I just continue with that term?*

A. You can certainly continue to call this meeting "Morning Meeting," particularly if you think your students will appreciate the continuity. But as a way to acknowledge the students' transition to the more adult responsibilities of middle school, consider introducing use of the term "Circle of Power and Respect"—or ask your students what they'd like to call the meeting.

The title "Circle of Power and Respect" marks a rite of passage for middle school students and lets students know that although the basic structure of the meeting remains the same as Morning Meeting, the focus and content will shift according to their changing developmental needs. Circle of Power and Respect appeals to the early adolescent need for a sense of power in their lives and their desire for respect. The title also reinforces the skills and values we want to teach—sitting in an inclusive circle and achieving personal power through respectful, assertive interactions with peers.

Q. *How do I introduce CPR so that students accept it? I'm afraid they'll think it's babyish.*

A. First, it's important to begin slowly, particularly if your students have not had any experience with Morning Meeting. Following are some points to keep in mind. For a more detailed discussion of these steps, take a look at the *Getting Started* discussion in the *"Overview"* chapter of this book, adjusting the pace and language to the developmental needs of your class.

- Explain what CPR is and why you think it's important. Emphasize the opportunities that CPR offers for peer contact. If students are unfamiliar with Morning Meeting, you might begin by saying something like, "This year we'll be starting the day with a meeting called Circle of Power and Respect. It's something that's done in a lot of middle schools as a way for students to get to know each other, to share their ideas, to practice skills, and to have fun together as a group. There are four parts: Greeting, Sharing, Group Activity, and Morning Message. Today we'll learn the first two."

- Phase in the implementation of the components. For example, have a Morning Message chart visible starting from the first day of school. Introduce simple greetings in the first week (*Appendix E*). Move carefully into Sharing, perhaps beginning with a focused sharing where each child gets to say one thing. Introduce group activities that are fun, active, and low risk (*Appendix F*).

- Be sure to model and practice necessary skills for each component. How do we greet each other in a respectful, friendly way? How do we speak concisely and clearly? How do we show that we're listening attentively?

- Choose and teach signals that will help manage the meeting—for example a raised hand as a signal for quiet.

- Discuss and teach the logistics of CPR. Where will you form your circle? How will students come into the circle? How should they sit?

- Generate ground rules with the students. Some examples of ground rules are to sit quietly when someone is speaking, be sure the speaker has finished speaking before you ask questions, raise your hand to speak, and be sure you have the group's attention before you begin to speak. You can begin a discussion of ground rules with a question such as "In order to make our CPR meeting respectful, safe, and fun, what rules will we need?"

- Establish clear consequences for breaking the ground rules and enforce them in a matter-of-fact and consistent way. For example, if a student

Circle of Power and Respect

carries on a side conversation while someone is sharing, that student might need to leave the group briefly. Be sure you stick to the consequences during the initial period of heavy testing.

- Take part in the group and let your enthusiasm show.

If your school has been doing CPR for a few years, you can also enlist the help of older students in the school to introduce CPR. Have eighth graders buddy up with an incoming class of sixth graders for one meeting a week. The older students can do a lot of the modeling and explaining. Seeing them actively engage in CPR gives it validity for the sixth graders.

Even with careful attention to how you present CPR, you might run into resistance from students who say it's too babyish. Keep in mind that at this age, what students say doesn't always represent what they want. You'll need to persevere, particularly if there's not a tradition of CPR in the school. And remember that many teachers have found that students miss CPR if it's not available, even though they've loudly complained about it.

Fine Tunings

Q. *What do I do with a student who's new to the class, particularly a student who is resistant to CPR and challenges the rules constantly?*

A. Welcome the student to the class and to CPR. Two suggestions on how to integrate the student into an established CPR routine are:

- Assign a buddy to help the student learn the ropes.
- Give the student an early opportunity to share about an interest or an area of expertise.

You may find that CPR gives the student the freedom to make a different—and better—choice about how to interact. But if the student can't or won't follow the ground rules, the student sits out and observes the meeting for a few sessions. If this doesn't work, then schedule a private conversation with the student and enlist the help of the guidance counselor or principal.

Q. *Some of my students live troubled, dangerous lives. What do I do if students share disturbing information?*

A. Some teachers feel it's safer to do focused sharings rather than single person sharings because this lessens the possibility of difficult information emerging.

Although there are times when this is appropriate, the risk is that students will never learn how to discuss difficult topics appropriately.

Early in the year, establish what is appropriate to share. After students have gotten comfortable with the routines of sharing, you can introduce a "hot topic" to give students experience in discussing difficult issues. Is there something controversial happening in the school or community? Frame an open-ended question that everyone can respond to. Use this as an opportunity to model and practice expressing and receiving different opinions respectfully.

In the same way, you can model and practice how to respond to difficult information. "How do we respond if someone tells us about something that makes them sad? Or something that scares them? What do you think would help that person? What has helped you when you've felt sad or scared?"

Be ready to intervene if needed. Intervention might take the form of asking an appropriate question, directing the conversation onto a less volatile or sensitive path, or ending the conversation. If you end a conversation, be sure that you talk with the student(s) individually as soon as possible.

Circle of Power and Respect

Q. *I've got too many other demands, particularly getting my students ready for state tests. How do I find time for CPR?*

A. Planning for CPR does take time. But it's time that pays off in the long run. In the *Middle School Guidelines,* Chip Wood says, "At the center of the CPR time...[is] the building of important skills of communication and cooperation and the creation of peer and adult support for each learner." He goes on to say that "it is clear that such time spent at the beginning of the school day actually saves instructional time later in the program." (Crawford 1998, 9)

Students who know, trust, and care for one another are supportive of all aspects of learning, including assessment. And CPR offers many opportunities to practice and reinforce skills needed to succeed in state assessment tests. For example, before achievement tests, students could share test-taking strategies that have worked well for them. Or the Morning Message chart can be used to reinforce test-taking skills or to review content. Group activities offer many opportunities to practice language arts, math, history, science, and other academic skills. And the routine of CPR will help students stay grounded and focused during the weeks of assessment.

Q. *What if I can't think of new activities and greetings?*

A. Keep in mind that your fellow teachers are a great resource. If you can, find a regular time to talk about what's happening in CPR and to share ideas for activities and greetings. And don't hesitate to cross disciplines. A language arts teacher might have a great word game that he could teach the math and science teachers and vice versa. Many teachers find it helpful to establish a system to help them remember what activities they've tried, how the activity went, and how they'd like to modify it in the future.

Also, in *Appendices E and F,* we offer many activities and greetings that are appropriate for various age levels. Feel free to use these and adapt them to your needs.

**Fine
Tunings**

A Silent Bulldozer of School Reform

Morning Meeting is a silent bulldozer in the field of school reform," proclaimed Maurice Sykes when he was deputy superintendent of the Washington, DC, public schools. I was happily predisposed to respect and accept his observations since I had often found him to be a master at crafting just the right phrase to describe essential notions as well as an astute observer of elementary classrooms.

This time, however, his metaphor just didn't sit well. A bulldozer? I closed my eyes and let the images of bulldozers I had known flow by. Dust…blistering yellow…noise…clanging…beep…beep…rubble. But wait, erase the clanging and beeping. Maurice had a different bulldozer in mind—a silent one. I tried to imagine it—this bright and powerful machine scooping and clearing and smoothing its way silently across the landscape.

The landscape in my imagination was a construction site, I realized. Construction. Hmmm. The word and its variants tumbled around in my head—construct, constructive, constructivist. I extended the metaphor as I began to think about the role of a bulldozer differently. Yes, it makes piles of rubble, but as a preface to clearing them away. It follows the wrecking ball and prepares the earth for new creation. New structures cannot be erected where old ones are still standing or where piles of debris litter the ground. Building requires a bulldozer.

I brought my interpretation to a group of colleagues who had come together for a discussion on Morning Meeting. What does Morning Meeting clear away, I wondered. And what is to be constructed in that clearing?

There were several moments of silence and then, around the circle, the responses came—eloquent and thoughtful every one.

"Morning Meeting clears time. The beginning of the school day is so often a jumble, kids doing seat work while teachers take attendance, do lunch counts. Morning Meeting makes time for teachers and children to be focused with each other on important things."

"And space. It clears a space for those things to happen. Making that space carries over, and it transforms the entire environment of the classroom."

"Morning Meeting clears away an old way of seeing children in a classroom to make way for a new approach. The new approach has children at its center and views community as a powerful instrument in teaching and learning."

Conclusion

"Morning Meeting clears away the barriers of social status and other inequities. Everyone's on the floor, on the same level, in a circle, looking at each other. Each morning it levels the ground, clears away yesterday's stuff and we start fresh. There are lots of opportunities for growth in the aftermath of a bulldozer's work."

"Yes, a bulldozer clears a space. And in that space can remain a hole, or an empty skyscraper full of unrentable space, or a sturdy, useful building. And it's work, filling in that space. We're always constructing. But Morning Meeting gives us the tools."

"Those tools, the simple strategies and clear structures, move us in the direction of profound goals. Sometimes we don't even know the full import of what's happening for a long time. That's the silent part."

It was a defining conversation. I looked around and summed up the years of teaching experience that the seven of us brought to the table. 135, I estimated. We wondered together, listened to each other, and built upon each others' ideas until a full new understanding emerged. Exploring my query in a social context had deepened and enriched both the process and its result immeasurably. It was, I realized with a jolt, just what Morning Meeting helps children to do.

Our meeting even mirrored the components of Morning Meeting, though without titles and overt structures. We had drifted in casually, saying our hellos to colleagues, smiles and nods of acknowledgment flowing back and forth and around the circle at our table. Greeting drifted into Sharing complete with questions and comments. I just can't get rid of this cough. How did the workshop in New Orleans go? The closing on your house is held up again? You must be so frustrated! And then on to our Group Activity—a planned and purposeful dialogue about Morning Meeting. And before we adjourned, some announcements: We'll reconvene at two o'clock. Remember to bring your calendars.

Some of us headed to our classrooms, some to another meeting, some back to our offices. Though the tasks that awaited each of us were different, we left invigorated and reminded of our common mission—our fascination with the process of learning and our passion for good schooling for all.

I remembered an observation by educator Suzanne Goldsmith that I had recently read in *Teaching Tolerance*. "Communities are not built of friends, or of groups of people with similar styles and tastes, or even of people who like and understand each other. They are built of people who feel they are a part of something that is bigger than themselves." (Goldsmith 1998, 4) Morning Meeting builds that kind of community.

Conclusion

Appendix A

What Children Are Learning in Each Component of Morning Meeting

Excerpted from *Morning Meeting Handbook,* compiled by Washington, DC, public school teachers enrolled in *Responsive Classroom* courses

Greeting

*When children are **greeting** each other, they are learning to:*

- Acknowledge the presence of themselves and others

- Recognize first and last names

- Be courteous, considerate, and caring

- Become more comfortable in a social situation

- Acknowledge different cultures

- Gain a sense of community and belonging

- Gain self-esteem

- Imitate words and motions

- Communicate clearly in an audible voice

- Remember games and words

- Make eye contact

- Wait their turn

- Pay attention and focus on the speaker

- Welcome classmates to the group

- Help classmates feel valued, liked, and wanted

- Practice self-control

- Understand spoken information

- Recall the sequence of sounds

- Use new vocabulary

- Use appropriate body language

- Develop new and different ways to greet each other

- Show respect for themselves and others

- Develop sequencing skills

Sharing

*When children are **sharing,** they are learning to:*

- Develop communication skills in expressive and receptive language

- Develop leadership skills

- Retell experiences in sequence

- Use critical thinking skills

- Organize ideas

- Identify the main idea

- Accept the values of others

- Respect the opinions, experiences, and cultures of others

- Become comfortable as the center of attention

- Select appropriate thoughts to share

- Ask respectful questions and give meaningful comments

- Express opinions

- Draw conclusions

- Make comparisons

- Distinguish between reality and fantasy

- Infer causes

- Take turns

- Pay compliments

- Build self-esteem

- Develop empathy and compassion

Group Activity

*When students are participating in a **group activity,** they are learning to:*

- Solve problems

- Think quickly and creatively

- Identify patterns and sequences

- Identify action words and directions

- Improve their gross motor skills

- Play and follow simple rules

- Empathize

- Increase muscle control, hand-eye coordination, and balance

- Increase self-confidence

- Use language creatively

- Participate in a variety of games and activities, both new and familiar

- Interact easily with classmates

- Repeat a message to others

- Participate actively in the group life of the class

- Participate in cooperative learning

- Learn through movement

- See the fun in learning and have a good time

- Support each other

Morning Message

When children are participating in **Morning Message,** *they are learning to:*

What Children Are Learning

- Participate in group oral reading

- Recognize letter sounds

- Recognize upper and lower case letters

- Recognize the names of classmates

- Follow directions and work independently

- Count, add, subtract, multiply, and divide

- Recall familiar words

- Identify rhyming words

- Identify and construct letters of the alphabet

- Write their own names

- Follow left and right progressions

- Identify verbs, adjectives, compound words, and pronouns

- Distinguish opposites

- Identify and use various punctuation marks

- Take responsibility for reading and spelling

- Distinguish picture clues and context

- Use letter names to represent sounds

- Build number concepts and problem-solving skills

- Strengthen predicting, sequencing, estimation, and probability skills

- Determine predictable chart patterns, configuration, sentence structure, and letter formation

- Use grammar properly

- Use information including seasons, months of the year, and days of the week

- Organize and plan

Appendix B

Letter to Parents about Morning Meeting

Here is a letter we have developed to provide information to parents about Morning Meeting. We strongly encourage you to adapt and edit it to meet your needs.

Dear Parents,

There's a wonderful new beginning to your child's school day! It's called Morning Meeting and it's a great way to build community, set a positive tone, increase excitement about learning, and improve academic and social skills.

Morning Meeting usually takes between twenty and thirty minutes. First thing each morning, the children and I gather in a circle. We begin by greeting each other. Every day, your child hears his or her name spoken by a classmate in a friendly and cheerful manner.

Next, a few students share some interesting news followed by a conversation with the class. This helps students listen carefully, think about what they hear, formulate good questions, and learn about each other. When children share, they have a chance to feel that their ideas are valued and that the other children care.

After sharing, there is an activity for the whole class. We might sing or recite a poem or play a math game. The activity time helps the class feel united as a group, reinforces academic skills, and helps the children learn how to cooperate and solve problems.

Finally, we read the Morning Message chart, which helps students think about the day ahead. Sometimes, I use this time to review and practice a reading, punctuation, or math skill.

Every day, Morning Meeting lets children know that school is a safe place where all children's feelings and ideas are important. We'd love to have you visit a Morning Meeting. Just give me a call to arrange a good time. You'll see for yourself why we're so excited about this start to our day.

Appendix C

Modeling: A Teaching Technique

Throughout this book, the technique of modeling is referred to as a teaching strategy. Generally, teachers use modeling when they want to teach a very specific behavior and want children to imitate the demonstrated way of behaving. It is frequently used to introduce children to expected behaviors during Morning Meeting: how to move chairs safely and efficiently; how to do a formal handshake; how to be a good listener, etc. Below is a step-by-step example of how a teacher might use this technique to teach children to pass a friendly handshake around the circle.

Step one: Teacher names and presents the desired behavior.

Example: "I want us to pass a friendly handshake. Watch what I do."

Step two: The desired behavior is demonstrated by the teacher.

Example: Teacher reaches over and shakes the hand of a student next to her.

Step three: Teacher asks students to notice and name the elements of the behavior. Teacher elicits the specific actions and expressions that made this a "friendly handshake."

Example: "What did you notice that made this a "friendly handshake?"
"You looked at Sean."
"You smiled."
"You turned your body so it was facing Sean."
"You took his hand."
"You said his name."
"What else did you notice about my handshake?"
"You shook his hand but not so hard."

Step four: The teacher focuses on "tricky" parts.

Example: The teacher might now focus more attention on the handshake itself since it's critical in this greeting that the physical contact be safe and positive. The teacher would repeat steps one through four, focusing on the handshake. "I want to be sure I give Sean a 'firm and gentle' handshake. Watch me."

"What made it 'firm'?"

"What made it 'gentle'?"

Step five: Students practice "tricky" parts by demonstrating and noticing what works.

Example: The teacher asks for students to demonstrate: "Who thinks they can give a 'firm and gentle' handshake?" The teacher then elicits observations from the children who are watching, for example, "What did you notice about the handshake Emily gave Becky?"

Step six: Students practice behaviors as a whole class.

Example: Teacher says, "Let's greet each other by sending a friendly handshake around the circle."

Step seven: Reinforce observed positive behaviors. This occurs both immediately following the modeling and at other points when desired behaviors are seen.

Example: "I saw people really look at each other. I heard names. I saw firm and gentle handshakes."

Step eight: Teacher continues to reinforce, remind, and redirect as needed. In addition to modeling desired behaviors, the teacher may at times want to playfully model "undesired" behaviors.

Example: The teacher takes hold of a student's hand by two fingers and asks, "Is this a firm handshake? Why not? Show me what I should do to make this a firm handshake."

Appendix D

Morning Meeting with Second Language Learners

By Bonnie Baer-Simahk

Bonnie Baer-Simahk is director of early childhood education for the Fitchburg, Massachusetts, schools and a consulting teacher for Northeast Foundation for Children. She has eleven years experience teaching English as a second language.

Many teachers know from first-hand experience that the number of students for whom English is a second language (ESL) is steadily increasing. These children come to the classroom with diverse cultural backgrounds and varying degrees of proficiency with the English language. As teachers, our challenge is to help these newcomers learn a new language and adapt to new cultural norms and behaviors. The predictable routines and rituals of Morning Meeting can help you welcome and support second language learners.

In this appendix you'll find suggestions for using the four components of Morning Meeting with second language learners. Each of the components can serve several purposes: welcoming the child, helping the child meet and become comfortable with new classmates, introducing and reinforcing language acquisition, and introducing and reinforcing new cultural norms and ways of behaving. The ideas can be used in any setting: a two-way bilingual classroom, an ESL classroom, or an inclusion classroom where second language learners join native speakers. Adapt the ideas to make them appropriate for your setting and age group.

Understanding Cultural Differences

In order to function well in this country, children from other countries need to develop comfort with American customs while maintaining pride in their native cultures. When you think about how to adapt Morning Meeting for use with second language learners, it's important to spend some time learning about the children's countries of origin so you can understand the particular challenges that each child might face. Although it's best to learn from the children and their families, some time spent in the library or on the Internet is also worthwhile. Here are some questions to ask:

- What are the traditions for greeting people in the child's culture?

- What has the child probably learned about how to behave towards adults? Towards peers? Towards children of the same gender? Toward children of a different gender?

- Is it culturally acceptable to touch another child? Is it culturally acceptable to make eye contact?

- What are the expectations regarding education for boys? For girls?

Knowing the answers to some of these questions will help you plan Morning Meeting structures that will ease the child's transition. And the child will feel appreciated and welcomed if you have taken the time to learn about family and cultural customs.

Morning Meeting with Second Language Learners

Greeting

Every culture has its own unique way of greeting people, and within each culture, subtle variations in the ways that people greet each other are often important indicators of status or respect. Newcomers understand that they will encounter new greeting practices in their new country. They might feel anxious about "getting it right" and about doing something that goes against what they've learned at home. The ritualistic nature of Morning Meeting Greeting can reduce some of this anxiety by easing children into the new norms and language.

Following are some greetings that are particularly helpful for second language learners:

Simple face-to-face greetings

These are good greetings for the beginning of the year or when a second language student has just joined your class. To offer these simple greetings, children need to learn a common phrase plus the name of the person next to them and be able to pronounce the name: "Good morning, Brian!"

Face-to-face greetings also involve nonverbal features that communicate friendliness in our culture—features such as a smile, suitable proximity, vocal volume, and eye contact. So, although the vocabulary demands are minimal, simple face-to-face greetings turn out not to be so "simple" after all! For example, some children have been taught at home to avoid eye contact with each other or, more often, with adults as an indication of respect. This is where your earlier research pays off by letting you know just how challenging these simple greetings might be for some second language learners. In order to adjust successfully to life in their new country, children will need to choose which social rules to use depending on the context. This will come easily in time for most children. But teachers can help by modeling and directing the newcomer's attention to other children who are greeting.

Ball toss or roll greetings

The child who is concentrating on catching and tossing a ball or beanbag is less likely to feel anxiety about English language skills. It is also easier to make eye contact when you must be sure that your classmate is ready before you toss the ball. Many teachers like to use a variety of balls and beanbags. Include some traditional balls from other countries, if you can find them.

Ball pass greetings

In some countries, hugging or shaking hands is a gesture of friendship. In other countries, it's not culturally acceptable to touch. In yet other countries, cross-gender handshakes are taboo, while same-gender friends greet each other with a kiss. Ball pass greetings, in which children pass a ball, beanbag, small stuffed animal, or other small object around the circle, can help children begin to feel comfortable with physically interactive greetings. And if you offer a variety of items, the greeting will help children build vocabulary. Precede the greeting by announcing the name of the item being passed. "Heeeeere's the rabbit. Good morning, Sasha!" To increase opportunities for syntax practice, add to or vary the sentences that the students use. For example, as you pass a pencil around, you could say, "Sasha needs a pencil. Good morning, Sasha." Sasha would then turn to Mike, handing Mike the pencil and saying, "Mike needs a pencil. Good morning, Mike."

Vocabulary is best learned in categories, so if you want children to learn animal names, you might begin by passing a toy rabbit, and the next day you might pass a dog. The next three days may find a stuffed cat, horse, and raccoon going around the circle. If you keep these animals available in a separate basket for a week or so, native speakers can use free time to review the names of the animals with the English language learners.

Be creative with the objects you pass around. You can use classroom tools such as pencils, pens, erasers, and rulers, or you can pass small figurines, toy cars, picture cards, refrigerator magnets, etc.

Greeting in each other's home languages

When classmates learn to greet in a classmate's home language, the second language learners gain a sense of belonging and the native English speakers gain some empathy into the difficulties of functioning in a new language. Learning greetings in a variety of languages can also turn out to be useful. How nice it would be for Fosia's mother, who stopped by the classroom, to be greeted by the "student greeter of the day" in her own language! *Appendix E* lists greetings in a number of languages. If you don't know how to say "hello" or "good morning" in the languages of your students, ask them or ask their parents.

Songs and chants

These greetings are wonderful ways for second language learners to become comfortable with new language forms. Often, phrases that are hard to say fluently are much easier when set to music. There are examples of talented singers who stutter when speaking, yet sing with beautiful fluidity. This same phenomenon applies to language learners.

The grid at the beginning of *Appendix E* will direct you to other greetings that work well with second language learners.

Sharing

At first, the Sharing portion of Morning Meeting, with all those incomprehensible words to decipher, might seem particularly daunting to second language learners. Although you wouldn't expect second language learners to share in the first week or two of school, you don't need to wait until they've gained fluency before they share. Remember that sharing doesn't need to be spontaneous speech. You or other students in the class can work with ESL students outside of Morning Meeting to help them prepare for sharing.

Sharing using props

After getting familiar with the format of sharing, the ESL students might try out a sharing in which they bring in a photo or an item from home, hold it up, and then respond to simple yes-and-no questions. As they begin to learn vocabulary, the supportive environment of sharing will give them wonderful opportunities to practice and to gain fluency.

Morning Meeting with Second Language Learners

Sharing classwork

Sharing class projects or artwork is a simple way for ESL students to participate in sharing. Prior to Morning Meeting, they can work with the teacher or a classmate to prepare and practice brief descriptive statements about the artwork or project.

Focus sharing

Whole-group focus sharing allows ESL students to hear many similar statements on the same topic. Again, students can prepare for this type of sharing outside of the meeting. A good format for a focus sharing is "Three About Me." Students choose three things to tell about themselves: "I like french fries. I have a brown dog. I play basketball." To make this easier, you can give students a fill-in-the-blank sentence format: "I like_____ ice cream. I come from _____. My favorite color is _____."

Appendix D

Theme sharing

ESL students can prepare for theme shares by studying related vocabulary ahead of time. For example, if the theme is "our family," students can study words such as "mother," "father," "sister," and "brother." Themes such as family, favorite foods/animals/places, sports, and celebrations are all popular. Some teachers have the children extend their learning by writing in a journal or doing home-work assignments based on the theme.

Group Activity

Group activities offer second language learners many opportunities to practice language in a relaxed and playful way. As with greetings, plan early group activities with both language skills and cultural comfort levels in mind. Here are several activities that work especially well with second language learners:

Who Has It

Distribute several toy animals around the circle. Not every student will have a toy. Students who receive toys should hold them where they are visible to every-one. The leader begins the activity by choosing anyone in the circle and asking a simple question, such as "Maria, who has the rabbit?" Maria then replies, "Darren has the rabbit." Darren then tosses the rabbit to Maria, who says, "I have the rab-bit." Everyone who has an animal then passes it to the person sitting to the right.

The person sitting next to the leader chooses someone and asks a question using the same structure as before: "Brenda, who has the (horse)?" "Tashira has the (horse)." Tashira tosses the horse to Brenda who says, "I have the (horse)."

And so on around the circle, until each person has asked the question, and each person has held at least one toy animal. The pace of this game can vary, depending on the comfort level of the speaker at any given time, becoming fast paced and energetic as fluency increases.

A note about using toys or props: ESL teachers typically use "realia" or "real stuff" in their teaching. Picture cards are frequently used, but three-dimensional objects, including toys and miniatures of all kinds, are even better. Many ESL students have had limited access to the variety of toys American children are exposed to and find them fascinating. And if you work in a mainstream classroom with older students, remember that they often like a lot of the same objects and activities as younger children so don't worry about using small toys as props

Morning Meeting with Second Language Learners

Beach Ball Vocabulary

This is a variation on Beach Ball Math (*Appendix F*). Place a picture sticker in each section of a beach ball. Toss the ball to a student across from you. The student looks at the picture sticker near where her hands are on the ball. The student names the item pictured and then uses that word in a sentence before tossing the ball to someone else.

Cooper Says

In an approach to language instruction called Total Physical Response, or TPR, students follow stated directions that involve a physical activity. This builds receptive language and allows students to respond to language in a low-risk way. In the activity "Cooper Says" the teacher, as "Cooper," issues instructions, which can vary depending on the language goals, and the students follow the instructions: "Stand behind the chair. Sit on the chair. Stand in front of the chair. Put your pencil on the chair."

The Word Game

This activity is most appropriate for an ESL class where all students are working at approximately the same level of language proficiency. Picture cards representing a category such as clothing, transportation, animals, or occupations are placed on the floor in the center of the circle. Each card is numbered and can be labeled with the name of the object as well. The teacher calls out a word, followed by a pause, and the corresponding number. "Blue pick-up truck…number twelve." "Red tractor…number five." Taking turns around the circle, students listen to the vocabulary word, select a card, and listen for the number to see if it is correct. Incorrectly identified cards go back on the floor. You can tape record the vocabulary words and numbers, with an appropriate pause between word and number. Using a tape rather than calling out the words and numbers adds challenge, since the students need to respond in a prescribed and unvarying amount of time. You can also add the rhythmic beat of a metronome or play music in the background to add excitement. Using the tape, an ESL student could do this activity at another time individually or in a small group.

Near and Far

This is a variation of "Hot and Cold," an old favorite that promotes language use in a playful and meaningful context. The student who is the first "seeker" covers his eyes, and an object is hidden in the room. The student then tries to locate it by asking questions such as "Is it somewhere in the meeting area?" Classmates give the seeker verbal clues such as "You're getting nearer… nearer…you're very near it." Or "You're far away."

The grid at the beginning of *Appendix F* will direct you to other activities that are good to use with ESL students.

Morning Message Charts

The Morning Message chart is a wonderful tool for developing literacy for ESL students of all ages. Be sure to use the chart to build vocabulary in a consistent manner. You may want to include a word of the day, challenging students to figure out the word's meaning from context clues. Or, when reading the chart as a group, you can stop frequently to ask students for definitions of words.

Here are a few additional points to keep in mind about Morning Message charts:

Copying the chart

ESL students can copy the chart each day in a loose-leaf book that can be used for individual language review. It's also good penmanship practice and can be a helpful and productive task when the rest of the class is engaged in activities that are incomprehensible or inappropriate for ESL students. Keep the chart simple, clear, and easy to read so students won't have trouble copying it.

Making mistakes

When you have ESL students in your classroom, be wary about the technique of "making mistakes" on the chart that students then correct. If the ESL students don't speak any English at all or have very limited English proficiency, they may be confused, thinking the "mistakes" are actually correct examples.

Cursive writing

Teachers of older students, who may use cursive writing on their charts, should stick to printing until ESL students' literacy skills are sufficiently developed. An ESL student who is just beginning to read English can become confused by exposure to print writing and cursive at the same time.

Appendix E

Morning Meeting Greetings

The grid on the following pages lists all the greetings that are in this appendix and indicates any special considerations, such as best time of year or most appropriate age group. The categories are:

Beginning of the year. These are greetings that are easy to teach and to do. Included are greetings that help children learn each others' names. These greetings can all be done later in the year as well.

Later in the year. These are greetings that take more instruction and practice in order to be done well. They work best a few months into the school year, once a sense of community and trust has been established.

Song, chant, or call and response. Some of these greetings are set to familiar tunes, as indicated in the description. Others might have tunes that you're familiar with from attending *Responsive Classroom* workshops. If you don't know a tune for a particular song, simply chant the words or make up a tune.

English as a Second Language (ESL). These greetings are particularly useful with second language learners. All of them provide safe ways for second language learners to meet their classmates and begin learning American customs; some also help build vocabulary and English fluency.

Younger. These greetings are most appropriate for use with grades K–3, although many of them can also be used with older students.

Older. These greetings are most appropriate for use with grades 4–8, although some of them can be adapted for use with younger students.

Academic. These greetings can be used to reinforce academic content and skills.

Morning Meeting Greetings

Title	Beginning of the year	Later in the year	Song, chant, etc.	ESL	Younger	Older	Academic
Adjective Greeting, p.158		■			■	■	■
African Greeting, p.158		■				■	
Alphabetical Greeting, p.158		■			■	■	■
Around the World, p.159		■		■		■	■
Backwards Name Greeting, p.159		■				■	■
Ball Toss Greeting, p.159	■			■	■	■	
Ball Toss Variations for Middle and Upper Grades, p.160	■			■	■	■	
Book Character Greeting, p.160		■			■	■	■
Brown Bear Greeting, p.160	■		■	■	■		
Butterfly Greetings, p.161	■				■	■	
Cheer Greeting, p.161		■	■	■			
Chugga Chugga, p.162		■	■		■		
Compliment Greeting, p.162		■			■	■	
Cross-Circle Greeting, p.162	■			■	■	■	
Different Languages for Greeting, p.162	■			■		■	■
Elbow Rock, p.163		■				■	
Formal Greeting, p.163	■			■	■	■	
Good Morning, Friends, p.163		■	■	■	■		
"Good Morning" Greetings, p.163	■	■		■	■	■	
"Good Morning" Greetings Using Props, p.164	■			■	■	■	■
Hello, p.164	■		■	■	■		

Title	Beginning of the year	Later in the year	Song, chant, etc.	ESL	Younger	Older	Academic
Hello, Neighbor, p.165		■	■		■		
Here We Are Together, p.165	■		■	■	■		
Hickety-Pickety Bumble Bee, p.166	■		■		■		
Hidey, Hidey, Hidey, Ho, p.166		■	■			■	
Hug Greeting, p.167		■			■		
____ Is Here, p.167		■	■	■	■		
Marbles Greeting, p.167		■		■	■	■	
My Name Is ____, p.167		■	■	■	■		
Name Card Greeting, p.168	■			■	■	■	
Number Greeting, p.168	■			■		■	
One-Minute Greeting, p.168		■			■	■	
One, Two, Three, Four, p.168		■	■	■	■		
On the List, p.169		■	■	■		■	
On the Phone, p.169		■	■	■		■	
Pantomime Greeting, p.169	■			■	■	■	
Quickie Righty/Lefty, p.170		■		■	■	■	
Rhythm Greeting, p.170	■	■	■	■	■	■	■
Rig-A-Jig-Jig, p.171		■	■	■	■		
Roll Call, p.171		■	■	■		■	
Silent Greeting, p.171		■		■	■	■	
Skip Greeting, p.172		■				■	■
Snowball Greeting, p.172		■		■	■	■	
Spider Web Greeting, p.172		■		■	■	■	
Where Is ____?, p.173	■		■	■	■		

Appendix E

Adjective Greeting

This greeting is appropriate to use with children who have studied adjectives and understand their use. To start the greeting, each student chooses an adjective that begins with the same sound as his/her first name and then introduces him/herself to the group by saying, "Hello, my name is *(adjective) (first name)*."

For example, "Hello, my name is Jazzy Janet!"

To make the greeting go more smoothly, you'll need to do some planning. Make a list of the initial letters or sounds of each student's first name. Then write down several adjectives that also begin with each of those letters or sounds. Bring this list with you to the Morning Meeting circle.

Before starting the greeting, take a few minutes to brainstorm with the children a long list of adjectives that you write on the board or chart. Guide students toward positive words. Add adjectives from your list as needed to ensure that there are several adjectives which begin with the initial letter or sound of each student's name.

Variation: If there's time, students often like the challenge of going around the circle a second time and trying to name each classmate, using the classmate's chosen adjective.

African Greeting

This greeting uses two phrases: "Sawa bona," which means "I see you," and "Sikhona," which means "I am here."

All members of the circle close their eyes. The person who begins the greeting opens his/her eyes, turns to the person to the right or left, says "Sawa bona, (neighbor's first name)." That student then opens his/her eyes and responds, "Sikhona, (greeter's first name)."

The greeting then continues around the circle until all members have been greeted.

Alphabetical Greeting

In this greeting, students say "Good morning" to each other in alphabetical order, being sure to use each other's first name. If students are just learning to alphabetize, it's best if you begin by greeting the student whose name comes first in the alphabet (or asking the students who should go first). With students who are more experienced with alphabetizing, you can begin anywhere in the circle. For example, if Lindsey is the first greeter, she greets Mark, who then looks for the person whose name would be next in alphabetical order. But when it gets to Will, he might find that he needs to go back to the beginning of the alphabet and greet Annie. This greeting can take a while to complete.

Around the World

You'll need an inflatable globe for this greeting. Students should have knowledge of continents and countries around the world. Each child will be sending greetings from some country or continent on the globe, so before the greeting begins, decide with the students how they'll select a country/continent. For example, they might say that wherever a child's right thumb lands when s/he catches the globe will be the country that child names. Or they might decide that each child chooses a place to name.

The child who begins the greeting says "Good morning, *(receiver's name)*" to another student in the circle, then rolls or tosses the globe to that student. The student who receives the globe responds by saying "Greetings, *(sender's name)*, from *(continent/country)*."

Backwards Name Greeting

This greeting gives students practice in sounding out unfamiliar words. Students write their first names backwards on a nametag that they wear. For example, Mike would write "Ekim" on his name tag. Going in order around the circle, students greet each other using their backwards names. For example, Jane would begin with "Good morning, Ekim." Mike would then say, "Good morning, Enaj," before turning to his neighbor to continue the greeting.

This greeting will be more fun and successful if you let students help each other or if you have the class begin the greeting by going around the circle and sounding out each student's name as a group.

This greeting may be confusing for students in your class who are just learning English or who have dyslexia.

Ball Toss Greeting

Each child greets another child, then gently throws, rolls, or bounces a ball to that child, who returns the greeting (but not the ball). S/he then chooses a new child to greet and to pass the ball to. The greeting continues in this way until each child has been greeted once. The greeting ends when the ball returns to the starter. If you're using a soft, small ball, throwing underhand works best. With a large, bouncy ball, rolling or bouncing the ball works best.

Ball Toss Variations for Middle and Upper Grades

Here are some variations which make the Ball Toss Greeting more challenging and more effective for building cooperation among older children.

Morning
Meeting
Greetings

- Pass the greeting ball around the circle as explained above. Now the ball goes around one more time silently (with no greeting or talking), repeating the pattern it just made. Children will enjoy doing it several times this way and competing against the clock.

- Pass the greeting ball as explained above. Then repeat, passing the ball silently in the same pattern. As the ball goes around, add one or two more balls at even intervals so that there are several balls going around in the original greeting pattern. Challenge the children to see if they can do it three times without dropping the ball or skipping anyone. You can also add the element of competition against the clock.

- Once the greeting ball has gone around the first time, have the children "undo the greeting pattern" by sending the ball back to the person who greeted them. This can be done with a greeting attached or silently. When the children get very good at remembering who greeted them, try ending your Morning Meeting with a ball toss in the reverse greeting pattern as students wish each other "Have a good day!" or whatever encouraging words the children decide they want to say that day.

Book Character Greeting

For a week, students wear name tags of their favorite book character. Greetings that week can be done using character names. At the end of the week, have students remove their name tags and see if they can remember each others' character names. This is a good greeting to do during Book Week.

Brown Bear Greeting

The student who begins the greeting turns to her/his neighbor, and the two students look at each other and smile while the group chants:

(First student's name), (first student's name), what do you see?

The first student then answers:
I see (second student's name) looking (or smiling) at me. Good morning!

The second student then turns to the next person and the chant repeats with new names.

After all students have been greeted individually, the whole group says:

Everyone, everyone, what do you see?
I see children looking (or smiling) at me.

Butterfly Greetings

There are two versions of this simple greeting:

- Sit-down butterfly—While saying good morning, two children sitting next to one another hook their thumbs together and wave their fingers in the sign language sign for butterfly. This greeting then goes around the circle.

- Stand-up butterfly—This is the same greeting except that students stand up and walk to greet someone across the circle.

Appendix E

Cheer Greeting

Going around the circle, students do the following call and response greeting:

Student: My name is *(first name)*.
Group: YEAH!
S: And I like to *(activity)*.
G: Uh-huh.
S: And I'll be a *(person who does this activity)*.
G: YEAH!
S: Every day of my life.
G: Every day of (his/her) life.

For example:

My name is Carla.
YEAH!
And I like to swim.
Uh-huh.
And I'll be a swimmer.
YEAH!
Every day of my life.
Every day of her life.

Chugga Chugga

The whole group stands and sings or chants the following words, greeting each child in the circle. The child who is being greeted participates in the "chugga" movements.

Hey there, *(first name of child being greeted).*

You're a real cool cat.

You've got a little of this *(Children in the group snap fingers.)*

And a little of that. *(Children in the group snap fingers.)*

So don't be afraid

To boogie and jam.

Just stand up and chugga

Fast as you can.

Chugga up, chugga chugga chugga chugga. *(Child being greeted jumps up.)*

Chugga down, chugga chugga chugga chugga. *(Child wiggles down.)*

To the left, chugga chugga chugga chugga. *(Child does the twist to the left.)*

To the right, chugga chugga chugga chugga. *(Child does the twist to the right.)*

**Morning
Meeting
Greetings**

Compliment Greeting

Each child greets another child and gives a compliment. Be sure to model how to give a compliment and set the expectation for compliments that reflect what children do, not what they wear or how they look.

Cross-Circle Greeting

Children greet someone sitting across the circle from them. There can be many variations on this, such as cross-circle boy/girl greeting, cross-circle someone-you-haven't-spoken-to-yet-this-morning greeting, etc.

Different Languages for Greeting

Some options:

- Bonjour (French)
- Buon giorno (Italian)
- Shalom (Hebrew)
- Buenas dias (Spanish)
- Ohaiyo (Japanese)
- Gutten morgan (German)

- Jen dobre (Polish)

- Jambo (Swahili)

- Kale mera (Greek)

- Sign language

- Asalam alakum (Arabic)

- Zao an (Chinese)

Elbow Rock

Created by a group of fifth graders, this is a variation of a simple handshake greeting. This greeting goes around the circle with each student saying good morning to the next, but instead of shaking hands, the students lock elbows and shake arms. This can be trickier than it sounds as students will often have difficulty deciding which elbow to offer and which elbow to aim for.

Formal Greeting

Students greet other students using last names: "Good morning, Ms. Cather," "Good morning, Mr. Loman." Students often enjoy being called (and hearing others called) by their last name.

Good Morning, Friends

The following chant is a good way to begin the Greeting portion of Morning Meeting but should not stand alone as the only greeting. After the class completes the chant, they can pass around the room a simple greeting that uses each student's name.

Good morning, friends.
Two words so nice to say.
So clap your hands,
And stamp your feet,
And let's start together this way.

"Good Morning" Greeting

This is the most basic greeting, making it a great greeting for the beginning of the year. Two students face each other, make eye contact, smile, and say, "Good morning, _____," using each other's first name.

Some variations to use early in the year:

- With a wave

- With a salute

- With a bow

- With a thumbs up

- With a peace sign

After a few weeks, when students are more comfortable with each other and with the format of Morning Meeting, you might add the following variations:

- With a handshake

- With a handshake that students make up

- With a high five

Morning   - With a high five and ankle shake
Meeting
Greetings   - With a pinky shake

- With a touch on the shoulder

- With an elbow shake

"Good Morning" Greeting Using Props

The basic "Good morning, _____," can also be varied by using props:

Variation one: Students pass a prop that's associated with an academic subject and greet each other using the appropriate title. For example, a student might pass a magnifying glass and say "Good morning, scientist *(student's first name)*," or pass a book and say "Good morning, reader *(student's first name)*." Props can be chosen to reinforce an academic focus for the day.

Variation two: Students pass a ball, beanbag, or small stuffed animal around the circle. This is a good greeting to use with second language learners because it can help students become comfortable with physically interactive greetings and it can help build vocabulary. Begin the greeting by announcing the name of the item being passed: "Here's the rabbit. Good morning, Sasha." Children then repeat this pattern as they greet each other.

Hello

As students chant or sing the following, they pass a handshake (or pinkie shake or high five, etc.) around the circle:

Hello, hello, hello, and how are you?
I'm fine, I'm fine, and I hope that you are, too.

Hello, Neighbor

Students form an inner and an outer circle. The inside circle faces the outer circle. Students who are facing each other are now partners who greet each other with the following chant. The inside circle then moves one person to the right so that everyone has a new partner and repeats the chant. This continues until everyone is back in her/his original place.

Hello, neighbor, what d'ya say? *(Wave to your partner.)*
It's gonna be a wonderful day. *(Arms circle over head and then move down to the sides.)*
Clap your hands and boogie on down. *(Clap hands and wiggle down.)*
Give me a bump and turn around. *(Gently bump hips.)*

Variation one: Instead of bumping hips, students can jump ("Give me a jump and turn around") or raise hands high ("Then raise your hands and turn around").

Variation two:
Hey there, *(partner's first name)*,
What d'ya say?
It's gonna be a dynamite day.
Grab your hands *(Partners join hands.)*
And circle around. *(Partners gently swing each other in a circle.)*
Reach real high *(Each person raises hands over head.)*
And boogie on down. *(Wiggle down.)*

Here We Are Together

The children sing the following song to the tune of "The More We Come Together." In line three, they follow the teacher's lead, filling in the names of each child in the circle. This can be done in several ways, depending on how far along children are in learning each other's names. Each child can say his/her own name; the teacher can sing alone, acknowledging each child; or the whole group can acknowledge each child.

Here we are together, together, together.
Here we are together all sitting on the rug.
There's _____ and _____ and _____ and _____.
Here we are together all sitting in room _____.

Repeat until each child is named.

Hickety-Pickety Bumble Bee

The whole class repeats the following chant until each child in the circle gets a chance to say his/her name.

Hickety–Pickety Bumble Bee.
Won't you say your name for me.
_____ *(Child says his/her name.)*
Let's all say it. *(Whole group says the child's name.)*
Let's clap it, too. *(Group says name and claps out the syllables.)*
Let's whisper it. *(Group whispers the name.)*
Let's turn off our voices and clap it. *(Group claps out the syllables without speaking.)*

Hidey, Hidey, Hidey, Ho

Morning Meeting Greetings

The following call and response asks individual children to fill in the blanks with two adjectives that describe "boogie"—for example, the "jumpin' jive boogey." Before doing this greeting, children might want to brainstorm a list of adjectives that they can choose from. The call and response continues until everyone in the circle has had a chance to be the "caller."

Child: Hidey, hidey, hidey, ho!
Group: Hidey, hidey, hidey, ho!
C: What d'ya say, what d'ya know?
G: What d'ya say, what d'ya know?
C: I got the _____ _____ boogie. *(Child who is greeting fills in the blank with two adjectives.)*
G: (S/he's) got the _____ _____ boogie. *(Group repeats the adjectives.)*
C: And I got it right now.
G: (S/he's) got it right now.
C: I'm gonna pick it on up. *(Child pretends to pick something up.)*
G: (S/he's) gonna pick it on up.
C: And pass it on along. *(Child pretends to pass an object to the next child in circle.)*
G: And pass it on along.
C: To my good friend _____. *(Child fills in with the name of the child who is being handed the "boogie".)*
G: To (his/her) good friend _____.
C: And (s/he's) got it right now.
G: And (s/he's) got it right now.

Now the second child begins the chant again with "Hidey, hidey, hidey, ho!"

Hug Greeting

Children gently hug the child they are greeting. Practice how to make eye contact before hugging and how to hug gently.

_____ **Is Here**

Children begin this greeting seated in the Morning Meeting circle. The child who starts the greeting stands up, turns to the next child in the circle, and offers a handshake. That child stands up to receive the handshake. While this is happening, the rest of the group begins to sing the following to the tune of "The Farmer in the Dell," filling in the name of the child who is being greeted:

_____ is here, _____ is here,

It's a great day because _____ is here. *(Children clap in rhythm.)*

The first two children remain standing while the second child passes the greeting to the third child in the circle, who also stands, and so on around the circle. The song continues until everyone is standing. The song ends when it comes back to the first child, who is greeted last. The greeting then closes with everyone clapping and singing:

We all are here. We all are here. It's a great day because we all are here!

Marbles Greeting

This is a quick greeting. Each student has three marbles (or other small objects). When the teacher says "Go," students mingle, greeting each other by saying "Good morning, _____." Every third person that a student greets gets a marble. When a student has given away all three original marbles, s/he sits down.

My Name Is _____

The child who begins the greeting turns to the next child in the circle and says the first three lines of this chant. The whole group then finishes the chant. During the last line of the chant, the two children shake hands. This pattern repeats as the greeting is passed around the circle.

Student: My name is _____ and
I'm here to say,
I hope you have a very nice day.

Group: Ooh ooh, ooh ooh ooh. *(First two beats are long, last three beats are short.)*

You like me and I like you.

Shake shake, shake shake shake *(First two beats are long, last three beats are short.)*

One, two, you know what to do. *(The two children greeting shake hands.)*

Name Card Greeting

Place name cards in the center of the circle. Turn over the top card. The student whose name is on that card begins the greeting. That student turns over the next card in the stack and greets that child. That child then turns over the next card, and so on. When all the cards have been used, the greeting ends with the last child greeting the first child.

Number Greeting

Place numbered slips of paper in a basket. Decide what numbers to use based on the size of your class and the size of the groups that will be greeting each other. For example, if you have twenty-four group members and you want pairs to greet each other, you'll number the slips one through twelve. If you have twenty-four group members and you want groups of four to greet each other, you'll number the slips one through six.

After each group member has drawn a number from the basket, you call out a number. Everyone holding that number comes to the center of the circle to greet each other.

One-Minute Greeting

This is a great greeting to use when time is limited. Students mingle and say, "Good morning, _____ ," to as many other students as they can in one minute. Emphasize the importance of standing still and making eye contact when greeting someone so that the pace doesn't get too frantic.

One, Two, Three, Four

This greeting can be sung or chanted. When a child's name is called, s/he comes into the circle and does whatever s/he wants as a movement—for example, a bow, curtsy, wave, dance, wiggle, etc. During the last line of the song, the child moves back to her/his place in the circle. Another child's name is called, and so on around the circle.

One, two, three, four, come on _____ hit the floor.

We're so glad you're here today.

Hurray, hurray, hurray!

On the List

The following can be sung or chanted. The child who is named in the third line stands up and does a movement such as a bow, wave, or dance step. Towards the end of the chant, that child sits down. The chant continues until every child in the circle has had a chance to stand up and move.

On the list, on the list,
Who's the next person on the list?
Since _____'s the next person on the list, *(Named child stands and moves.)*
S/he'll tell you a story, now dig this!
When you're up, you're up.
When you're down, you're down.
If you don't greet *(next child in the circle),* you're up-side-down!
Side down…side down!

Appendix E

On the Phone

In this call and response, the group begins by calling a child's name. That child responds. At the end of the call and response, the first child names another child in the circle. The chant continues until every child has been named.

Group: Hey there, _____ .
Child: Someone's calling my name.
G: Hey there, _____ .
C: Must be playing a game.
G: Hey there, _____ , you're wanted on the phone.
C: Since it's my friend, *(another child in circle),*
    tell her/him I'm at home.
G: Just sitting on the sofa watching the clock.
    Go tick tock, tick tock de wawa.
    Tick tock, tick tock de wawa wa!

Pantomime Greeting

The child who begins the greeting pantomimes something about him/herself (favorite activity, favorite food, favorite sport). The whole class then greets that child by saying "Hello, _____" and then mimics the pantomime. This continues around the circle until all children have been greeted.

Quickie Righty/Lefty

When pressed for time, this "quickie" greeting can come in handy. One student begins by saying "Good morning, everyone." The class responds in chorus, "Good morning." Each child then greets the person on either side of him (waiting as needed for the person to be available). The one important rule is that students have to make eye contact with the person they're greeting. This ensures that everyone will feel greeted and acknowledged.

Rhythm Greeting

With your students, establish a four-beat rhythm by snapping fingers, clapping, or slapping hands on knees. In time with the rhythm, everyone says:

Say your first name.
When you do,
We'll say your first name back to you.

Morning Meeting Greetings

The student who begins the greeting then says his/her first name on the first beat. The group snaps or claps beats two, three, and four, and says the student's first name on the next beat (beat one again):

Student: "Johnny" *(two, three, four)*
Group: "Johnny" *(two, three, four)*

Now the group repeats the opening chant, "Say your first name…" Johnny's neighbor then says her/his first name, and the group repeats it, and so on around the circle.

Variation one: As a way for the class to learn everyone's full name, each student can say his/her last name and the class can respond with the student's first name:

Say your last name.
When you do,
We'll say your first name back to you.
Student: "Porter" *(two, three, four)*
Group: "Johnny" *(two, three, four)*

Variation two: When the class has learned everyone's full name, have each student say his/her first name and the group respond with the student's last name:

Say your first name.
When you do,
we'll say your last name back to you.

Student: "Johnny" *(two, three, four)*
Group: "Porter" *(two, three, four)*

Rig-A-Jig-Jig

Half of the class makes an inner circle and the other half makes an outer circle. The inner circle moves around while the outer circle stays still or moves in the opposite direction. Everyone sings the following song. When the verse ends, the people in the inner circle greet the people across from them in the outer circle. This continues for several rounds.

A rig-a-jig-jig and away we go,
Hi ho, hi ho, hi ho.
As I was walking down the street,
Down the street, down the street,
A friend of mine I chanced to meet,
Hi ho, hi ho, hi ho.

Roll Call

This is a call and response greeting. Individual children name themselves, then say their nickname, and finally choose another designation, such as "student," "soccer player," or "friend."

Group: Roll call, check the beat, check, check, check the beat.
　　　　Roll call, check the beat, check, check, check a-begin.
Child: My name is _____.
G: Check!
C: They call me *(nickname)*.
G: Check!
C: I am a *(role designation)*. That's what I am.
G: That's what (s/he) is.

Silent Greeting

One child greets another silently using a part of his/her face (eyebrows, eyes, mouth, etc.) or a part of his/her body (arms, shoulders, legs, etc.) but without making any physical contact. This greeting can be used in several formats: greeting around the circle, across the circle, or a quick right/left greeting.

Skip Greeting

In this greeting, the child who begins announces the number of spaces that will be skipped. For example, the child says "Skip four" and then walks to the fifth person in the circle and greets him/her. The greeter then takes that person's place and the student who was greeted walks to the fifth person down, greets, and switches places, and so on until everyone has been greeted. The greeting will flow around the circle several times. Before the greeting begins, work with the class to figure out how many spaces to skip based on the number of people in the circle that day. The challenge is to make sure that everyone gets greeted.

Snowball Greeting

Morning Meeting Greetings

Each student writes his/her name on a sheet of paper and crumbles it up so that it looks like a snowball. Students then toss the crumbled pieces of paper into the center of the circle. Students pick up a snowball that has landed near them and open the paper. The student who begins the greeting then walks over to the student whose name s/he has and says "Good morning, _____." The first student returns to his/her place in the circle and the student who was greeted finds the student whose name is on his/her snowball and greets that student, and so on until everyone has been greeted.

Variation: After the initial round of greetings, students recrumble the papers that they're holding and toss them. Each student picks up a new snowball, reads the name, and then respectfully watches that student for the rest of the day, with a goal of noticing something positive about the student. At the end of the day, the class circles up and each student pays a compliment to the classmate s/he observed all day.

Spider Web Greeting

The child who begins the greeting holds a ball of yarn. The child greets someone across the circle and gently rolls the ball to that person while firmly holding on to the end of the string. The person who receives the ball of yarn greets another child across the circle and rolls the ball of yarn to that student, making sure to hold onto the unraveling strand with one hand. This continues until everyone has been greeted and the yarn has created a web across the circle. To unravel the web, children greet each other in reverse order until the ball of yarn is wound up again.

Where Is _____ ?

This call and response is sung to the tune of "Frere Jacques," filling in a child's name in the first line.

Group: Where is _____? Where is _____?
Child: Here I am, here I am.
G: How are you today sir/ma'am?
C: Very well, I thank you.
G: We're glad you're here, we're glad you're here.

Appendix E

Appendix F

Morning Meeting Activities

The grid on the following pages lists all the activities that are in this appendix and indicates any special considerations, such as best time of year or most appropriate age group. The categories are:

Beginning of the year. These are activities that are easy to teach and to do. Included are activities that help children learn each others' names. These activities can all be done later in the year as well.

Later in the year. These are activities that take more instruction and practice in order to be done well. They work best a few months into the school year, once a sense of community and trust has been established.

English as a Second Language (ESL). These activities are particularly useful with second language learners. All of them provide safe ways for second language learners to become part of the classroom community and begin learning American customs; some also help build vocabulary and English fluency.

Younger. These activities are most appropriate for use with grades K–3, although many of them can also be used with older students.

Older. These activities are most appropriate for use with grades 4–8, although some of them can be adapted for use with younger students.

Academic. These activities can be used to reinforce academic content and skills.

Morning Meeting Activities

Title	Beginning of the year	Later in the year	ESL	Younger	Older	Academic
Alibi, p.178		■			■	
Alphabet Story, p.178		■		■		■
Aroostasha, p.178	■		■	■	■	
Aunt Minerva, p.179		■				
A Warm Wind Blows, p.179	■		■	■	■	
A What? p.180	■				■	
Beach Ball Math, p.180		■	■	■	■	■
Beach Ball Vocabulary, p.181		■		■	■	■
Beach Ball Vocabulary for ESL, p.181		■	■	■	■	■
"Bingo," p.181	■		■		■	
Boppity Bop Bop Bop, p.181		■			■	
Buzz, p.182		■	■	■	■	■
Categories, p.182		■			■	■
Category Circle, p.182		■		■	■	
Category Snap, p.183		■		■	■	
Caught Red-Handed, p.183	■		■		■	
Clapping Names, p.184	■			■		
Cooper Says, p.184	■		■	■	■	
Coseeki/Follow the Leader, p.184	■		■	■		
Description, p.184		■			■	■
Description: A Variation on Twenty Questions, p.185		■			■	■
Don't Make Me Laugh, p.185		■		■	■	
Encore, p.185		■				
Famous Pairs, p.186		■			■	■
Fact or Fiction, p.186	■			■		
Find a Place, p.186	■			■	■	
Four (or Five) Songs, p.186	■			■	■	
Fruit Game, p.187	■				■	
Gesture Name Game, p.187	■			■		
Grandmother's Trunk, p.187		■			■	
Guess the Number, p.187		■	■	■	■	■
Guess the Word, p.188		■		■	■	■

Title	Beginning of the year	Later in the year	ESL	Younger	Older	Academic
Hands Up for '02, p.188		■			■	■
Hot and Cold, p.189	■		■	■	■	
Human Protractor, p.189		■	■	■		■
Improv, p.189		■			■	
Incorporations, p.190	■			■	■	
I See, p.190	■			■	■	
Match-Up, p.190		■	■	■		■
Memory Name Game, p.190	■			■	■	
My Bonny, p.191	■				■	
Nonverbal Birthday Lineup, p.191	■		■		■	
Oliver Twist, p.191	■		■		■	
"One-to-Ten" Math Game, p.192		■			■	■
Pantomimes: *Group Charades*, p.192		■		■	■	■
Magic Box, p.192		■		■	■	
Occupation Pantomime, p.192	■			■	■	
One Thing You Like to Do, p.193	■			■	■	
Pantomime This Object, p.193	■			■	■	
What Are You Doing? p.193		■		■	■	
Pass the Mask, p.193		■		■	■	
Pass a Sound, p.193		■	■	■	■	
Patterns, p.193		■			■	
Pica Fermé Nada, p.194		■			■	■
Pop, p.195		■		■		■
Popcorn Name Game, p.195	■		■	■		
Ra-de-o, p.195		■			■	
Rainstorm, p.196		■	■	■	■	
Sparkle, p.196		■			■	■
Telegraph, p.197		■		■	■	
Telephone, p.197		■		■		
Three Question Interview, p.197	■		■		■	
What Did I Do?, p.198		■	■	■	■	
Who Has It?, p.198		■	■	■	■	
Zip, Zap, Pop, p.199		■		■	■	
Zoom, p.199		■		■	■	

Appendix F

Alibi

Choose one student to be the detective. S/he leaves the room. While the detective is out, the group decides on a crime that has been committed, then chooses a student to be the guilty party and a student to be the spokesperson. The detective comes back into the room and joins the circle. The spokesperson tells the detective what crime has occurred. Now the detective asks each player in the circle for his/her alibi—"Where were you at the time of the crime?" Going around the circle in order, each player gives a brief, one-sentence alibi. The detective listens carefully and then asks for the alibis again. Going around the circle in the same order as before, each player must give the exact same alibi using the exact same words except for the child who was chosen as the guilty party. The guilty party changes his/her alibi just slightly. For example, the first time perhaps the guilty one says, "I was at the doctor's." And the second time the guilty one says, "I was at the dentist's." The detective gets three attempts to guess who the guilty person is and then a new detective is chosen.

Alphabet Story

The first person in the circle starts to tell a story with a sentence beginning with the letter "A": "Aunt Helen came to my house the other day," for example. The next person in the circle continues, adding a sentence that begins with "B": "Buddy, her terrier, came with her." The class continues through the alphabet until everyone has added to the story.

Aroostasha

Students stand in a circle with their hands clasped in front of them, fingers interlaced.

Begin the activity by demonstrating the chant and body movements. To do this, chant "Aroostasha, aroostasha, aroostasha-sha" while moving your clasped hands from the right side of your body to the left and pulsing your hands up and down to the beat. Then do the chant while moving your hands back to the right side of your body, pulsing to the beat as you go. Have your class repeat the chant and body movements after you.

Call out "thumbs up," then chant and do the above movement with hands clasped and thumbs up. Call out "thumbs up, wrists together." Do the chant and movement with hands clasped, thumbs up, and wrists together. Call out "thumbs up, wrists together, elbows in." Do the chant and movement with

Morning Meeting Activities

hands clasped, thumbs up, wrists together, and elbows in. By now your class should be able to do the movements as soon as you call out the instruction without first having to see you demonstrate.

Keep going in this manner, adding one body position at a time. For example, you can add:

- Knees together

- Toes in

- Bottom out

- Tongue out (Ever try to say "Aroostasha" with your tongue out? Kids will really get a laugh out of this!)

Aunt Minerva

The child who begins the activity decides on a category such as "hot" but does not tell anyone else. Instead s/he gives several examples to demonstrate the category by telling things that Aunt Minerva likes and doesn't like. For example, if the category is "hot," s/he might say, "Aunt Minerva likes Florida but doesn't like Alaska. Aunt Minerva likes heavy down quilts but doesn't like thin sheets. Aunt Minerva likes soup but doesn't like ice cream." The other players try to figure out the category. When they know the category, they give an example of something Aunt Minerva likes and doesn't like. The child who began the activity acknowledges whether the guesser is right or not about what Aunt Minerva likes and doesn't like. The leader keeps giving examples and listening to others' guesses until many of the children have the category.

To keep this activity from feeling frustrating, end one round and begin another before there are only a handful of children still guessing.

A Warm Wind Blows

Move chairs into a circle. The number of chairs should be one less than the number of participants. Participants sit in the chairs and one person stands in the middle of the circle. S/he says "A warm wind blows for anyone who _____," filling in the blank with a category such as "has a dog." Everyone who fits that category comes into the center of the circle and then quickly finds a new place to sit. The one person who doesn't find a seat now stands in the center of the circle and says "A warm wind blows for anyone who _____," naming a new category. The activity continues for several rounds.

This lively activity is a great way for children to learn about each other and to see what they have in common with classmates. Encourage students to name categories that relate to interests, hobbies, and family rather than clothing or appearance. You could brainstorm a list of categories before beginning the activity.

A What?

This activity requires two small objects such as balls or beanbags. The first person hands one of the objects to the next person in the circle and says, "This is a _____," filling in the blank—for example, "This is a potato." The receiver says, "A what?" The first person replies, "A potato." The receiver says, "Oh, a potato," then passes the object to person number three, repeating, "This is a potato," and so on.

Morning Meeting Activities

After the "potato" gets started around the circle, begin passing the second ball in the opposite direction, giving it a different name. "This is an eggplant." "A what?" "An eggplant," and so on. When the items meet in the middle, things can get pretty chaotic. The goal is to pass both items completely around the circle. You can also make up nonsense names for the items.

Beach Ball Activities

Multi-paneled beach balls can be used in a number of activities that reinforce academic skills. Instructions here are for math, language arts, and ESL. But with a little creativity, the activity can be adapted for many subject areas.

Beach ball math

Before doing the activity, write a number on each panel of a beach ball. Be sure to include the small circles at the top and bottom.

Begin this activity by choosing (or having a student choose) a math function, such as addition, subtraction, multiplication, or division and then tossing the ball to someone else in the circle. The person who catches the ball looks at the numbers beneath her/his hands. These numbers become an equation that the child tries to solve using the designated function. For example, if the function is multiplication and the student's hands cover a three and a seven, the student then needs to multiply three times seven and give the correct answer. The student can ask for help if needed. Once the equation is solved, the student tosses the ball to someone else in the group.

Beach ball vocabulary

Instead of numbers, write vocabulary words on each panel of a beach ball. The student who catches the ball needs to define one of the words near where his/her hands are and use it correctly in a sentence.

Beach ball vocabulary for second language learners

Place picture stickers on each panel of a beach ball. The student who catches the ball looks at the stickers under or near her/his hands. S/he needs to name one of the items and then use that word in a sentence.

"Bingo"

Begin by creating "Bingo" cards on sheets of 8 1/2 x 11 paper. Each square on the card will contain a fact that could apply to several students in the class. For example, "Has a cat," "Favorite color is blue," "Has more than three siblings," "Speaks a language other than English," etc. Students can suggest facts or help you create the cards.

Give each student a card. Students then mingle and try to find classmates who match the various facts. When a match is found, the student who has been identified signs that square. For example, when Shawna finds out that Juan has a dog, Juan signs that square on Shawna's card. Each student can only sign one square per card. The goal is to fill the card.

Boppity Bop Bop Bop

Before doing this activity, decide with the students on movements for several three-person and one-person scenes. For example, a three-person scene might be called "elephant." The middle person waves an arm up and down like a snout, and the other two people use opposite arms to make ears. Another three-person scene is "cowboy," in which the middle person circles an imaginary lariat and yells "Yahoo!" and the two side people tap their knees like a galloping horse. A one-person scene is "Elvis," in which the person swivels his/her hips like Elvis.

One student ("it") stands in the middle of the circle. S/he points to someone in the circle and names a "scene." If s/he names a three-person scene, the person pointed to and the people to either side must do the prearranged movements before "it" says "Boppity bop bop bop." If "it" names a one-person scene, everyone must do the movements before "it" says the phrase.

Anyone who doesn't complete the movement before "it" completes the phrase, moves to the center of the circle and becomes "it." If several people don't complete the movement, they all come to the center of the circle. They decide together what the next scene will be, point, and chant "Boppity bop bop bop."

Buzz

Going around the circle, students count from one to a hundred. Whenever a student comes to a number that contains a seven or is a multiple of seven, s/he says "Buzz" instead of that number. For example, 1, 2, 3, 4, 5, 6, buzz, 8, 9, 10, 11, 12, 13, buzz, 15, 16, buzz, etc. Move quickly. If someone makes a mistake or pauses too long, s/he skips a turn.

Variation: Play "Fizz," which is the same activity except that the number is five instead of seven. This makes the activity easier for younger children. Or try "Fizz-Buzz": 1, 2, 3, 4, Fizz, 6, Buzz,...

**Morning
Meeting
Activities**

Categories

Choose (or have a student choose) a category such as rivers, state capitals, or cars Working in small groups, students have a limited amount of time to brainstorm as many examples as they can for the named category. For example, if the category is rivers, students might come up with "Mississippi, Rio Grande, Nile, Ohio, etc." Someone in the group should write down the answers, and someone should be the spokesperson.

When the time is up, ring a bell or use some other prearranged signal to stop the action. Children form a circle. The spokesperson for each group says how many items are on his/her group's list. The spokesperson for the group with the longest list then reads his/her group's list. Other groups check off any of the first group's items that appear on their lists. Then other groups can read the additional items that weren't on the first group's list.

To vary the activity or add challenge, students could guess what items are left after the first group reads their list or they could play a version of Twenty Questions.

Category Circle

Children stand or sit in a circle. One child goes into the center with a ball (Nerf ball, beanbag, anything easy to catch and pass). The child turns around three times, stops, and tosses the ball to someone standing across from him/her. The child who catches the ball names a category and immediately starts passing the ball to the person on the right who continues passing the ball. The child in the center tries to name as many items in the category as possible before the ball is passed all the way around to the child who started the category. Another child can be assigned to count how many items in the category are named.

Category Snap

The group sits in a circle. The leader starts a rhythm using a sequence of knee slap, hand clap, right-hand finger snap, left-hand finger snap. The leader then announces a category, such as fruits, on the right-hand finger snap and names an example, such as apples, with the left-hand finger snap. The next person in the circle must be ready to name the leader's fruit with the right-hand finger snap and then a new example in that same category with the left-hand finger snap: Knee slap, hand clap, "apples, apricots." The play continues around the circle. Once an item has been named, it cannot be used again.

Variation: The category is announced before the activity begins. Each person chooses and says out loud an item that belongs in that category. Once an item has been named, it can't be used again. The leader begins by identifying his/her own item with the right-hand finger snap and then names another player's item with the left-hand finger snap. That player then names her/his item followed by another player's item and so on. This variation sends the action jumping around the circle and demands that children not only listen but also remember what other players said.

Caught Red-Handed

For this activity, you'll need two or three (or more) small objects that can be easily passed around the circle, behind children's backs. One person stands in the middle of the circle and closes his/her eyes for a moment. Children who are in the circle begin to pass the objects behind their backs, as sneakily as possible. They also pretend to pass objects so that at all times students are either passing an object or faking a pass. The person in the middle opens his/her eyes and tries to figure out where the objects are in the circle. The person has three guesses, which should be made quickly.

Variation: Place a ring on a string that is long enough to go all the way around the inside of the circle. Children hold the string with both hands and pass the ring or pretend to pass the ring to each other while the child in the middle tries to guess who has the ring.

Clapping Names

In this activity, children will clap out the number of syllables in each child's first name while they chant the name. You can begin with your own name, chanting the name and clapping once for each syllable. Then either go around the room or ask children to volunteer to be next. You can vary the activity by having children clap out last names or self-chosen nicknames.

This is a good activity to do at the beginning of the year when children are learning each other's names. It is also a good activity to do if a new child joins the group later in the year.

Cooper Says

The leader is "Cooper." Cooper gives the group instructions. Group members follow the instructions only if the instructions are preceded by "Cooper says ..." For example, if the leader says, "Cooper says touch your toes," group members touch their toes. However, if the leader says, "Touch your toes," group members stand still. Keep the activity moving quickly. You can increase the difficulty by challenging the group to follow ten directions correctly.

This activity is similar to "Simon Says," except that no one is ever "out."

Coseeki/Follow the Leader

One player leaves the group and stands where s/he cannot see the group. The group chooses a leader who does a movement, such as tapping his/her toe, which the others follow. The leader changes the movement regularly and the others follow the leader's movement. The hidden player returns, stands in the middle of the circle, watches the movements, and tries to guess who the leader is.

Variations:

- Send more than one player away and have them confer.
- Limit the guesses.
- Have two leaders, who take turns starting new movements.
- Use movements that make no sound.

Description

In this activity, three students describe an object in the room while the rest of the class tries to guess the object. You can choose the object or you can let the three children choose. The object needs to be fairly complex and be visible to everyone else, such as the classroom bulletin board, and the three children need to give different descriptions. Give the three students time to meet and decide what each will say. When they return to the group, they give their descriptions, and the rest of the group tries to identify the object.

Children need to listen carefully, concentrating on what is being said. They also need to focus on the details of a complex object. This activity might generate a discussion about how there are several ways to see things. It can also lead into a creative writing exercise.

Description: A Variation on Twenty Questions

This activity is similar to Twenty Questions. The group sits in a circle. The child who is "it" gets a card with a word written on it taped to his/her back. The word names a person, place, or thing; the word can be related to subjects the class is studying, such as fish, mountains, rivers, capitals, books. The child can ask the class up to ten yes-or-no questions to try to determine what is written on his/her back. To increase the difficulty, the group can agree ahead of time that certain questions or types of questions are not allowed. Each time a question is asked, the class responds with thumbs up to indicate "yes" or thumbs down to indicate "no." The child can make a guess at any time with a maximum of three guesses. After ten questions, the child can ask for clues from the class before making a final guess.

Don't Make Me Laugh

Two students stand in the center of the circle. One student's job is to stay silent and straight-faced. The other student's job is to make the first student laugh, using funny facial expressions and gestures. Students participate in this activity on a volunteer basis.

Encore

This is a fun and quick activity that calls for teamwork. Children divide up into several teams based on where they are sitting in the circle. The teacher calls out a word or topic (examples: rain, dancing, rivers, farm animals, etc.), and within five minutes (or less), each team tries to come up with as many songs as it can that use that topic or word.

Before doing this activity, take some time to think about songs that relate to different words, just to ensure that you don't pick a word that's impossible to match to a song.

Famous Pairs

Make a list of famous pairs of people, such as Lewis and Clark, Abbott and Costello. You could brainstorm a list with the class. Write these names on cards, one name to a card, then tape a card to each student's back. Students mill around, asking each other questions to determine what name is on their back. Then they find the person who has their partner's name.

Fact or Fiction

Morning Meeting Activities

A student tells three things about him/herself—two facts and one fiction. For example, the student might say, "I've been to France. I play the tuba. I've got three cats." Going around the circle, everyone makes a guess about which claim is fiction. The student then says which students guessed correctly, and someone else takes a turn.

Find a Place

All the children silently think of a place in the room. As the teacher counts from one to five, each student walks to the place that s/he thought of. The teacher counts from one to five again, and each student walks to a new place before the teacher reaches five. Then students return to their first place, hopping on one foot, while the teacher counts to five. Students next return to their second place, hopping on the other foot, while the teacher counts to five. The class can continue, varying the movements—for example, skipping, walking backwards, jumping like a frog, etc. Older children can do this activity using three or four places.

Four (or Five) Songs

Before the activity begins, write the names of songs on cards, one song to a card. Each student will need a card. Choose the number of songs based on the number of students in class that day and on the size groups you want students to end up in. For example, if you have twenty-four students and you want them to end up in groups of three, you'll choose eight songs and write each song on three cards. Be sure to pick songs that everyone is likely to know.

To begin the activity, distribute the cards. Students then mill around, humming the song that's written on their card. When they meet up with other students humming that song, they form a small group. The activity could end with each group singing a verse of their song.

Fruit Game

Each person in the circle names a piece of fruit, with no repeats. Then, covering teeth with lips, one child says his/her own fruit followed by another child's fruit—for example, "apple, mango." The child who initially named "mango" goes next, attempting to say "mango" plus the name of yet another child's fruit without showing any teeth, and so on. It is very difficult for children not to laugh and show their teeth in this activity. Students who do show their teeth simply stop saying anything and just watch the action, which is almost as much fun. The activity has no definitive end; you may want to start with a time limit so that it doesn't go on too long. In addition to being a lot of fun, this activity reinforces listening skills.

Gesture Name Game

Children stand in a circle. Each child says his/her name while making a gesture for each syllable in the name. For example, Jill Bishop might clap her hands for "Jill" and snap the fingers of first the right hand and then the left hand for "Bishop." The group then repeats her name and her gestures. The activity continues around the circle.

Grandmother's Trunk

Begin the activity by saying "I'm going on a trip, and I need to pack my grandmother's trunk." The first child then says what s/he will pack in the trunk. For example, "I'm going on a trip, and I'm taking my bike." Each child in the circle then adds one item to the trunk. "I'm going on a trip, and I'm taking my bike and my sneakers." "I'm going on a trip, and I'm taking my bike and my sneakers and a baseball." And so on around the group.

Guess the Number

Think of a number and write it down on a piece of paper that you hide. Let students know that you've chosen a number between one and _____, choosing a number range that appropriately challenges the group, given their age and skill level. Going around the circle, students take turns asking a yes-or-no question to try to determine the number. If a student does not have a question, s/he may "pass." A student who thinks s/he knows the number may take a guess. If the guess is incorrect, the questioning continues. If it's correct, the teacher may choose another number or pick a child to choose a number. To emphasize the cooperative nature of this activity, be sure that the child who correctly guesses the number is not the next one to choose a number. The ultimate goal of this activity is to see how many numbers the group can figure out within a certain period of time.

Encourage students to think of questions that will give them information about the number, rather than questions that just eliminate one number. Instead of asking if it's the number after fourteen, for example, students might ask if it's a two-digit number, whether it's larger than ten, or if it has a five in it.

This activity helps children develop questioning skills and listening skills.

Guess the Word

Give students a list of words, grouped by kind—for example, nouns, verbs, adjectives, and adverbs. You choose a word from the list and write it down on a sheet of paper that you hide. Going around the circle, students ask questions that first narrow the possibilities to the kind of word and then to the correct word. Students may pass if they want to. A student who thinks s/he knows the word may take a guess. If the guess is incorrect, the questioning continues. If the guess is correct, another word is chosen and another round of the activity begins. As with the activity Guess the Number, be sure that the child who correctly guesses the word is not the one to choose a new word.

Hands Up for '02 (change for correct year)

Name a category and choose a child to begin the activity. (Once children are familiar with this activity, they can name the category and start the round.) The whole group begins the following chant, filling in the name of the category in the fourth line. The last line names the child who is beginning the activity. Going around the circle, each child then quickly names an item in the category. If a child misses by repeating or taking more than a few seconds, the activity starts over again with the chant, naming the child who is next in the circle. The object is to get all the way around the circle without a miss.

Morning Meeting Activities

Hands up / / *(silent beats)*
For '02 / / *(silent beats)*
Gonna' name *(clap, clap)*
Some _____ *(clap, clap)* *(A category is named, such as rivers, states, animals, etc.)*
One apiece *(clap, clap)*
No repeats *(clap, clap)*
No hesitation *(clap, clap)*
No duplication *(clap, clap)*
Starting with *(clap, clap)*
_____ *(Fill in with child's name, and child says something that fits in the category.)*

Hot and Cold

Select an object to hide. Choose one child to be the "seeker" and send that child out of the room. Hide the object in a place that is difficult enough to provide a challenge but not so difficult that the search becomes frustrating. The group can help you choose a hiding place. Invite the seeker back into the room. The seeker begins looking for the object. The group guides the search by saying "hot" whenever the seeker gets near the object and "cold" whenever s/he moves away from the object.

If you have second language learners in your class who might be confused by this use of "hot" and "cold," the group can say "near" and "far."

Human Protractor

Everyone stands in a circle, hands touching toes. Tell children that they are going to straighten up gradually, keeping their arms straight out in front of their bodies. At the same time, they'll be counting to twenty, so that by twenty their hands are reaching towards the sky. Children will need to remember where their hands are at different numbers. Then you call out numbers between one and twenty, and the group assumes the position for each number. When children are familiar with the activity, they love being the leader.

Improv

Two students go to the center of the circle and start acting out a simple scene, such as eating at a restaurant, doing homework together at school, etc. At any point, someone from the circle can call out "freeze." The two people freeze while the person who called out goes into the center and takes the place of one of the actors by putting his/her body in the exact same position. The two in the center now act out a different scene that makes sense for the positions that they are starting in.

Incorporations

In this activity, students will form and reform groups as quickly as possible. The leader hits a gong or rings a bell and then gives directions for forming groups, such as "Get into groups of three." The leader hits the gong again and gives a different direction: "Get into groups where everyone is wearing something the same color." The activity moves very quickly.

I See

Morning Meeting Activities

Begin the activity by saying "I see!" The class responds, "What do you see?" You then describe something, such as "I see bubbles floating in the air." The students act out that idea until you again say "I see." All the students stop again and respond, "What do you see?" The activity continues with you or a student leader suggesting other ideas.

Choose movements that suit your students. Older children will probably not want to be "bees buzzing around," but they may enjoy pretending to be rock-and-roll stars or star athletes. Try calling out movements that move from the very slow to the very active and back to the slow again to end the activity.

Match-Up

Before doing this activity, print a short nursery rhyme, poem, or song on a sheet of paper. Make a few copies of the page and cut them into strips, with one line on each strip. You'll need enough strips that each child can get one strip.

To begin the activity, distribute the strips of paper. The first child stands and reads from his/her strip. Other children who have the same line raise their hands and these children form a small group. Continue until every line of the poem/song has been read. After the children have formed groups, do a complete reading of the poem, starting with the group who has the first line.

Memory Name Game

Ask a simple question, such as "What is your favorite color?" Each child in the circle says his/her name, answers the question, and then repeats what each preceding person said. For example, the first child might say, "Patricia, red." The second child would say, "Tim, orange; Patricia, red." The third child would say,

"Nancy, blue; Tim, orange; Patricia, red." It's important to keep the question simple and the answers brief. Younger students can just repeat what the person immediately preceding them said. This is a great activity for reinforcing listening skills and for learning names.

My Bonny

Everyone sings the song "My Bonny Lies Over the Ocean." Whenever words beginning with a "b" are sung, children alternate between sitting and standing. *For example:* "My Bonny *(stand)* lies over the ocean. My Bonny *(sit)* lies over the sea…"

The words to the song are:

My Bonny lies over the ocean.
My Bonny lies over the sea.
My Bonny lies over the ocean,
So bring back my Bonny to me.
Bring back,
Bring back,
Oh bring back my Bonny to me, to me.
Bring back,
Bring back,
Oh bring back my Bonny to me.

Nonverbal Birthday Lineup

Challenge the children to line up according to their month and day of birth, without any talking.

Oliver Twist

The whole group chants the following song and does the accompanying movements. Begin slowly, then speed up until children are all laughing as they try to keep up.

Oliver twist, twist, twist *(hands on hips and twist body)*
Can't do this, this, this *(tap right foot and shake forefinger of right hand)*
Touch his head, head, head *(touch head with hands)*
Touch his nose, nose, nose *(touch nose with hands)*
Touch his ears, ears, ears *(touch ears with hands)*
Touch his toes, toes, toes *(touch toes)*

"One-to-Ten" Math Game

This activity begins like Human Protractor (page 189): Students stand in a circle touching their toes. To a slow count of ten, they straighten up until they are standing with hands reaching for the sky. Let students know that they need to remember where their hands are at each number. Once the group is all upright, the leader calls out a math problem whose answer is a number between one and ten—for example, "ten minus two." The rest of the group responds "eight" and assumes that position. You can use whatever range of numbers is most appropriate for the group.

Pantomime Activities

Following are several activities that involve pantomiming. In each of these activities, it's important to remind children that they need to wait until the pantomime is finished before they start to guess what's being pantomimed.

Group Charades

Choose a fairly broad category, such as animals, simple machines, geology, etc. Students gather in small groups. Each group gets a topic within the category. For example, if the category is animals, one group might get dogs, another might get cows, and so on. Each group takes about five minutes to figure out how to act out this topic without using words, sounds, or props. All students in the group work together. For example, all students act out one dog rather than each student acting out a dog. When groups are ready, they come back together in a circle, and each group acts out its topic. Other students try to guess what the topic is.

Magic Box

Place an imaginary magic box in the center of the circle. The first child goes to the box and takes out an imaginary item, then uses that imaginary item to pantomime an activity. When a child in the circle thinks s/he knows what the activity is, that child silently goes to the center and joins in. The originator says whether the guess is correct or not. Then those two children sit down and another child takes something out of the box, and the process continues.

Occupation Pantomime

Children take turns pantomiming an occupation, such as house painter, while others guess what the occupation is.

One Thing You Like to Do

Each child in the circle pantomimes a favorite activity, and then the group guesses what that activity is.

Pantomime This Object

Choose a real object, such as a broom, and use it to pantomime something else: a guitar, a horse, a violin, etc. The group guesses what the object is that you're pantomiming. Then pass the object around the circle. Any child who wants can pantomime something with it while the group guesses what the object is.

What Are You Doing?

In this activity, one person goes to the center of the circle and mimes some simple action such as brushing one's hair. The next person in the circle approaches the hair-brusher and asks, "What are you doing?" The hair-brusher responds by saying something completely different such as "I'm washing the floor." The person who asked now pretends that s/he is washing the floor. The next person from the circle then comes to ask the floor-washer, "What are you doing?" This goes on until everyone in the circle has had a chance to mime an action.

Pass the Mask

The person who begins the activity makes a face, then "passes" that expression on to the next person in the circle. That person first imitates, then changes the first expression and passes the new expression on to the next person, and so on around the circle.

Pass a Sound

This is a variation of Pass the Mask. The first person makes a sound and passes it to the second person, who first imitates and then gradually changes the sound. The second person then passes the new sound to the third person, and so on around the circle.

Patterns

Allow plenty of time for modeling and for doing this activity. One person goes out of the room. The rest of the group decides on a pattern for how they will answer questions. For example, they might decide that everyone will answer for the person to the left, that everyone will answer for one person in the circle, or that everyone will answer for the person who is asking the questions. Once the pattern is set, the child returns to the room and begins to ask individuals yes-or-no questions in an effort to figure out the pattern. The child might ask a question like "Are you wearing sneakers?" If the pattern is that everyone will answer for Claire, and Claire is wearing sneakers, then anyone asked that question will say "yes." If a group member does not know the answer to a question, s/he must venture a guess anyway. For example, if everyone is answering for Claire and the questioner asks, "Do you have a brother?" there will be some people who do not know whether Claire has a brother. If the answer is incorrect, anyone in the group who knows the true answer calls out "Pattern!"

The questioner should ask questions that s/he already knows the answer to, should ask questions rapidly, and should ask as many people as possible. The job of the questioner can be very challenging, so you may want to have two people working together as questioners. This is a good activity to save until later in the year when students know each other well.

Pica Fermé Nada

This is a cooperative strategy activity. A person starts the activity by thinking of a number with an agreed upon number of digits (the number of digits is based on the age and skill level of the children playing). The person writes that number on a piece of paper, which is put aside until the end of the activity.

Next, the leader, using chart paper or the chalkboard, writes a blank for each digit of the number: _ _ _ for a three-digit number, for example. The object of the activity is for the rest of the class to work together to figure out the number by suggesting other three-digit numbers. Each time a number is suggested, the leader responds with information about whether the numerals in the suggested number are in the "mystery" number and whether they are in the right digit place. The information is provided in the following format:

- Pica (P) means the numeral is in the mystery number but is not in the correct place.

- Fermé (F) means the numeral and place are correct.

- Nada (N) means the numeral is not in the mystery number at all.

For example, if the mystery number is 386 and someone suggested 365, the leader would write down "365 — F P N." Then the next person in the circle would suggest a number based on this information. Any child who wants to pass may do so.

Morning Meeting Activities

The activity continues in this fashion until someone is ready to name the number. When naming the number, the child must also explain the thinking that solved the mystery.

To help build a cooperative spirit, the rules allow children to ask for strategic thinking help before suggesting a number. Other children may also offer strategic thinking help even if it's not asked for. However, the guesser is not obliged to ask for or accept such help.

The more challenging way to do this activity is for the leader to write the Pica, Fermé, and Nada symbols with no direct relationship to the placement of the numerals in the suggested number. For example, if the mystery number is 386 and a student suggests 365, the leader might write "N F P." If another students suggests 357, the leader might write "N F N." The random placement of the symbols makes the strategic thinking more challenging and fun.

Pop

Choose (or have a student choose) a number – for example, five. Going around the circle, the children count "one, two, three, …" until they get to five. The fifth child in the circle pops up and says "Pop." The counting then starts over. This goes around and around, with the counting skipping over the children who have already popped, until everyone in the circle is standing. Variations include popping for even numbers, odd numbers, multiples of certain numbers, etc.

Popcorn Name Game

Children go around the circle, popping up like popcorn and saying their name, for example, "Hi, I'm Jeff," then sitting back down again. Children should pop in order, one at a time.

Ra-de-o (Radio)

The class forms a circle with room to form another circle on the outside as the activity progresses. Each syllable of the word "Ra-de-o" has a specific arm and hand gesture that goes with it and determines where the action will be sent next. One person starts by saying "Ra" and puts either the left or right hand above the head, pointing to the person on either the immediate left or right. That person says the next syllable, "de," and puts either the left or right hand under the chin, pointing to the person on either the immediate left or right. The next person says the last syllable, "o," and points to anyone in the circle, who then starts the action all over again by saying "Ra."

Any player who makes a mistake comes out of the inner circle and begins to form the circle of "hecklers" on the outside of the inner circle. The hecklers' job is to use words and sounds to try to distract the other players. Hecklers may not stand in front of players or use their arms or hands to obstruct the players. Instead, they may talk incessantly in a player's ear; they may sing at the top of their lungs; they may tell jokes or stories, etc. Pretty soon most players will be on the outside heckling, and only a few will be on the inside trying to pass the actions. The activity can end before it gets down to one last player.

Rainstorm

Begin the activity by making motions and noises that sound like a rainstorm. The children imitate you, continuing to make that motion/sound until you change to a different one. The rainstorm motions and noises are:

a) Raise both hands in the air with palms out, wriggle the fingers, and at the same time, make a soft whooshing noise with the mouth.

b) Rub the palms of the hands together repeatedly.

c) Click the fingers.

d) Clap hands on thighs, alternating the left hand and right hand.

e) Clap hands on floor or, if playing outside, stomp feet.

f) Loudly clap hands together.

A storm that builds from soft to hard rain to thunder and lightning and back again will take the pattern a→b→c→d→e→f→e→d→c→b→a.

Variation: Begin the activity with a rainstorm motion, then pass that motion by turning to the person immediately to the left and making eye contact. That person passes the motion to the left and so on around the room. When the motion reaches you again, begin to pass the next motion. Each student continues to make the old motion until a neighbor passes along a new one.

Sparkle

Students stand in a circle. Announce (or have a student announce) a spelling word, such as "energy." The first student in the circle repeats the word. The next student uses the word in a sentence. The following students spell the word, one letter per student. When the word has been correctly spelled, the next student in line waves his/her hands in the air and says "Sparkle!" and then sits down. A new word begins and follows the same sequence.

If a student makes a mistake in spelling, for example, s/he puts an extra "n" in "energy," the next student in the circle can say "check." If that student does not catch the mistake, others in the circle can say "check." (If no students catch the mistake, you need to step in and say "check.") The student who made the mistake can then either correct the mistake or ask for help from the group (a "lifeline"). Once the mistake has been corrected, the activity proceeds.

Telegraph

Children stand in a circle, hold hands, and close their eyes. The first child (or the teacher) chooses a nonverbal message, such as three quick, gentle hand squeezes, and sends it to the next child. That child sends the message to the next student, and so on around the circle. After the message goes around the circle, the last child explains verbally what it was. The message can also be sent in both directions until one child receives it from both sides.

Telephone

Children sit in a circle. The first child (or the teacher) whispers a simple message into a neighbor's ear. For example, "I like chocolate." That child then whispers the message into the next child's ear, and so on around the circle. The last child in the circle says the message out loud, and everyone notices whether or not the message changed. (It usually does.)

If you'd like to use this activity to practice good listening and speaking skills, then follow the first round with a discussion. Ask children what helps them to hear a message correctly. Write answers on chart paper or the board. Then send a new message around, reminding students to use good communication skills so that the message doesn't get garbled. If the message is still garbled, then you can try a third round in which children check with each other to be sure they heard the message correctly.

Three Question Interview

Each child in the circle should have pencil and paper. Have children pair up with a child they don't know very well. The children in the pairs interview each other, asking three simple questions, such as "What is a movie that you like?" or "What do you like to do after school?" The person asking the questions can jot down his/her partner's responses. When both people have had a chance to ask three questions, they find other partners and repeat the process.

After fifteen to twenty minutes, or when each person has had a chance to interview several others, everyone returns to the large circle. Go around the circle. Each child says his/her name, and then you say, "What do people know about _____?" People who interviewed that child share what they learned. Allow time for each person to have a turn.

Variation: This variation works well early in the year, particularly if there are second language learners in the class. Each child interviews a partner and then introduces the partner to the group, using the following fill-in-the-blanks statements:

"This is my friend _____
and her/his favorite activity to do is _____."

You could substitute the following for favorite activity:

- Favorite book
- Favorite food
- Something the child is good at

What Did I Do?

One child stands in the middle of the circle. The rest of the children look closely at the child. That child then leaves the circle and, without being seen by the group, changes one thing about his/her appearance. For example, the child might tuck in a shirt, roll up pants legs, unbutton a sweater, etc. The child then returns to the circle, and others try to guess what has been changed.

You can vary the amount of time allowed for observation and/or the number of things changed (to two or three things). You can also have children change some things in an area of the classroom rather than something about themselves. Or you can have children do this activity in pairs, with one partner changing something and the other guessing what has changed. The important thing is that this remains a fun activity that reinforces close observation and does not become competitive.

Who Has It?

This is a good activity for second language learners since it repeats a simple sentence structure and allows them to practice vocabulary words within a category.

Distribute several toy animals around the circle. Not every student will have a toy. Students who have toys hold them in their laps where the toys are visible to everyone. The leader begins the activity by choosing anyone in the circle and asking a simple question, which will be repeated in the same format throughout the activity. "Maria, who has the rabbit?" Maria then looks around the circle and answers, "Brian has the rabbit." Brian tosses the rabbit to Maria who says, "I have the rabbit."

Everyone who has an animal now passes it to the person sitting to the right. The person sitting next to the leader chooses someone and asks, "Brenda, who has the dog?" and the activity continues until each person in the circle has asked the question and each person has held at least one animal.

Zip, Zap, Pop

One student in the circle begins by placing his/her hand on top of the head, fingers pointing either right or left and says "Zip." The person who receives the zip can either continue the zip on to the next person in the circle, or can place hand under chin, pointing back towards the initiator, and say "Zap," or can point at someone across the circle and say "Pop." And the activity continues from there.

Variation one: One student stands in the center of the circle, points to someone in the circle and says "Zip." People on either side of the person who got "zipped" point to each other and say "Zap. " The trick is that they need to say "Zap" before the person in the middle says "Pop."

Variation two: One person ("it") stands in the center of the circle, points to someone in the circle, and says either "Zip," "Zap," or "Pop" and then counts quickly to eight. If "it" said "Zip," the person pointed to must say the name of the person to his/her right before "it" reaches eight; if the word was "Zap," the person must name the person to the left; if the word was "Pop," the person must say his/her own name. If the person doesn't say the appropriate name before "it" reaches eight, that person becomes "it."

Zoom

The person who begins the activity says "Zoom!" and turns his/her head quickly to a neighbor on either the right or left. That person passes the zoom to the next person and so on around the circle. You can challenge the group to go faster and use a stopwatch to time them.

Variation: Explain that the word "Eek!" stops the zoom and makes it reverse direction. For the next round, allow one Eek! and then in subsequent rounds increase the number of Eeks! allowed. Remind children that the goal is to get the Zoom passed all the way around the circle. If only a few children have had a chance to say Eek!, you can end the activity by having everyone say Eek! together.

Recommended Resources for Group Activities

The following resources are available from Northeast Foundation for Children, 800-360-6332, ext. 151 or 413-772-2066, ext. 151, www.responsiveclassroom.org:

Morning Meeting Activities

Davis, Andy, Peter Amidon, and Mary Alice Amidon, eds. 2000. *Down in the Valley: More Great Singing Games for Children.* Brattleboro, VT: New England Dancing Masters Productions. Booklet and CD.

Feldman, Jean. 1995. *Transition Time: Let's Do Something Different.* Beltsville, MD: Gryphon House.

Gregson, Bob. 1982. *The Incredible Indoor Games Book.* Carthage, IL: Fearon Teacher Aids.

Harrison, Adrian. 2002. *36 Games Kids Love to Play.* Greenfield, MA: Northeast Foundation for Children.

Luvmour, Sambhava and Josette Luvmour. 1990. *Everyone Wins!* Gabriola Island, BC: New Society Publishers.

Northeast Foundation for Children, eds. 1998. *16 Songs Kids Love to Sing.* Greenfield, MA: Northeast Foundation for Children. Book and audio cassette/CD.

Paton, Sandy and Caroline Paton. 1975. *I've Got a Song!: A Collection of Songs for Youngsters.* Sharon, CT: Folk Legacy Records. Booklet and audio cassette.

Paton, Sandy and Caroline Paton. 1989. *When the Spirit Says Sing.* Sharon, CT: Folk Legacy Records. Coloring book and audio cassette.

Pirtle, Sarah. 1998. *Discovery Time for Cooperation and Conflict Resolution.* Nyack, NY: Creative Response to Conflict, Inc.

The following resources are available from Origins, 612-822-3422, www.OriginsOnline.org:

Cunningham, Patricia and Dorothy Hall. 1994. *Making Big Words: Multilevel, Hands-On Spelling and Phonics Activities*. Carthage, IL: Good Apple. For older children.

Cunningham, Patricia and Dorothy Hall. 1994. *Making Words: Multilevel, Hands-On, Developmentally Appropriate Spelling and Phonics Activities*. Carthage, IL: Good Apple. For primary grades.

Spolin, Viola. 1986. *Theater Games for the Classroom: A Teacher's Handbook*. Evanston, IL: Northwestern University Press.

The following resource is available from the publisher, 800-567-6772, www.newsociety.com:

Bodenhamer, Gretchen, Leonard Burger, Priscilla Prutzman, and Lee Stern. 1988. *The Friendly Classroom for a Small Planet: A Handbook on Creative Approaches to Living and Problem Solving for Children*. Gabriola Island, BC: New Society Publishers.

Appendix F

Appendix G

Suggestions for Creating Morning Message Charts

Elements of the Morning Message Chart

When you create your Morning Message charts, think about including the following:

Friendly greeting

The chart often takes the form of a letter. Begin the chart with a salutation such as Dear Students; Dear Fine Fifth Graders; Good Morning, Cooperative Class; Dear Biologists; Dear Wonderful Writers; etc.

Date and day of the week

You can vary how you write this. For example, if students are learning days of the week, leave the day of the week blank so that they can fill it in. Or if students are learning different ways to write the date, give them space to write the date in this format: __/__/__.

Focus

It's a good idea if each of the elements of the chart connects to a single focus. For example, if you want to focus on math, you could begin the chart with "Dear Marvelous Mathematicians." In the interactive task, students could solve an equation. If you want to focus on some aspect of community building, you might begin the chart, "Good Morning, Friendly Students." The interactive task might be "Write one adjective that describes a friend," followed by a thinking question: "What's one thing you can do to be a good friend today?"

Interactive task

Include a task that students respond to, either on the chart or during discussion. Leave adequate space on the chart for students to write or draw their answers. To define the space where students write their answers, draw a balloon shape or a circle (or some other creative shape). If you ask yes-or-no questions or ask students to choose among several choices, include a grid where students can write their names. Allow time for discussion of students' responses.

Here are some examples of interactive tasks with an **academic focus:**

- "Should we have uniforms in school? Be prepared to share your thinking."

- "Write one good adjective to describe a puddle."

- "Write one adjective that describes a good friend."

- "Punctuate the following sentences."

- "Find and correct spelling mistakes in today's message."

- "Here are scrambled words from your spelling list. Your spelling challenge is to unscramble them! Write the correctly spelled words below."

- "Write an equation that equals today's date."

- "Between 1 and 10, how many prime (or odd or even) numbers are there? List your guess below."

- "List one fact you know about Dr. Martin Luther King, Jr."

- "We will review division. Who remembers what $\overline{)}$ means?"

You could also:

- Write a message about an upcoming classroom event but leave out all periods or all capitals. Ask students, "What is wrong with this message? How would you correct the message?"

- Leave out words or letters throughout the message and ask students to fill them in.

- Present a math word problem.

- Write a summary of a controversial local issue. Ask students, "Do you agree or disagree? Use the grid to record your response. Be prepared to share your thinking."

Here are some examples of interactive tasks with a **community building focus:**

- "We need to remember our rule for keeping recess safe and fun. Think of one way you will keep it safe. Write your answer below."

- "We will have visitors from _____. How can we welcome them?"

- "Write one word that describes how you felt about your day yesterday."

- "Here's a riddle. 'Who in this class likes to draw?' Write your answers below." or "Here's a riddle. 'Who in this class has the middle name Rose?' Write your answers below."

- "What's your favorite time of day? Sign your name on the grid below."

- "What's your favorite toy? Print your name on the grid below."

News, reminders, directions

Use the chart to share an important piece of news (visitors, special assemblies, birthdays, student achievements, etc.), reminders (classroom rules, name of Greeting leader and doorholder, classroom responsibilities, etc.), and administrative directions (permission slips, homework, project sign-up, etc.).

Appendix G

Special Topics

Some teachers plan their charts so that there's a focus linked to each day of the week. This varies content, ensures that there's a focus, and contributes to predictability.

Monday: Weekend

- "Think of one thing you did over the weekend that was fun…interesting…challenging…exciting…hard…etc. Write a brief response below."

- "How did you spend your weekend? Write your name on the grid."

Read a book or saw a movie	Played a game	Visited a new place	Played sports	Visited friends	Other

Tuesday: Math

You can make up problems from real-life situations, surveys, and curriculum material. For example:

- "If we order pizza for our class party and everyone gets two slices, how many pizzas do we need? (What other information do you need to solve this problem?) Write your answers below and be prepared to share your thinking."

- "Fill in the grid with your name if you have a pet. What fraction of our class does not have a pet?"

Dogs	Cats	Birds	Gerbils	Other

Suggestions for Creating Morning Message Charts

Wednesday: Humor　　*Brainteasers*

Use riddles, jokes, cartoons, doodles...

For example:

"Hey, class..."
"What?"
"What do you do with a blue elephant ???"
"We don't know."
"Try to cheer him up !!!"

Thursday: Language Arts

Use word games, poetry, songs, unscrambling words, similes, Twenty Questions, etc.

For example: "Here's a familiar phrase: 'Madam I'm Adam.' Read the phrase backwards. Now what does it say? How many other words can you think of that are the same whether you write them left to right or right to left? Write some examples below."

Friday: Current Events

Use headlines, articles, pictures, the newspaper, etc., to initiate a discussion about relevant news. May also lead to class debates about ongoing issues.

Appendix H

Sample Morning Message Charts

Pre-kindergarten

Good Morning!

Laura is first.

Raymond is the doorholder.

Today is Monday.

We will fingerpaint.

Good Day, Children!

Thomas is first.
Maria is the doorholder.

Today is Thursday.

Do you like pizza?

Yes	No

Kindergarten

Sample Morning Message Charts

Good Day!

Laura is first.
Raymond is the doorholder.

Today is Monday, October 2, 2001.

We will paint.
What is your favorite color?

Red	Blue	Green	Yellow	Black	Other

Good Day, Children!

Thomas __ first.
Maria __ the doorholder.
Today __ Wednesday,
February 12, 2002.

We will write a story about our
trip to the store. Draw a food
that you saw at the store.

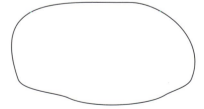

First Grade

Dear Children,

Laura is _irst.
Raymond is the _oorholder.
_oday is Friday,
November 16, 2001.

Today we will talk about our spider.
Write one thing you observed
about our spider.

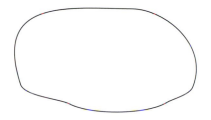

Good Morning, Mathematicians!

Thomas is first.
Maria is the doorholder.
Today is Friday,
February 8, 2002.

Write a math equation for "8."

Be ready to share your thinking.

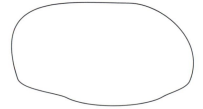

Second Grade

**Sample
Morning
Message
Charts**

good morning, Friendly Workers

Today is monday, january 28, 2002.

Laura is first and Raymond is our Greeting leader

yesterday we talked about how to invite someone to join in an activity with you. today we will practice. who remembers some friendly actions that you might use? Write your ideas here:

What's wrong with today's message?

Good Morning, Authors:

Today is ____, _____ __, ___.
The shortcut way to write the date
is __/__/__.

Laura is first and Raymond is our Greeting leader.

We will be reading our published books to the kindergartners after lunch. Each of you will have a partner to read to. What are some questions you can ask your partner to help you talk about the story?

Third Grade

Good Morning, Weather Watchers! Today is Wednesday, March 7, 2002, and Sam will lead our Greeting.

Yesterday we learned about four types of clouds and today we'll be drawing them. What do you observe about today's clouds?

Challenge Question: Can you name one type of cloud? Be ready to share at meeting.

Appendix H

Thursday, Nov. 16, 2001

Dear Friendly Workers,
I am wondering what you know about compliments. Please share your thinking. What is a compliment?

What would a compliment sound like? Write some examples of compliments below.

Thank you for your ideas!

Fourth Grade

**Sample
Morning
Message
Charts**

April 25, 2002

Dear Awesome Artists,
The illustrations you did for our class
"read-aloud" book are fantastic! They
show the rich variety of ideas and
feelings you had about the book.
I would like to display all of them.
Let's brainstorm some interesting
ways that we might arrange this
display. Put your suggestions here:

Be thinking if you would like to be
a curator for this display.
Have a great learning day!

2/10/02

Dear Multiplying Mathematicians,
Wow! You have been multiplying up
a storm the last few days! We will
continue the same multiplication
work today. Here's one sample for
you to try: 7 x 45 = _____. Bring your
answer to meeting and be ready to
tell what you did to solve it. We need
more multiplication problems for us to
solve later. Write one example below:

Fifth Grade

5/I/02

Good Morning, Adventurers!
Last week we were really engrossed in
our wagon train game. The Donner
Party definitely had a difficult and
disagreeable journey!

While preparing this game, you've
had to make some critical decisions to
ensure that you make it to Oregon.

What has been your most challenging
decision so far? Be ready to tell why
this decision was hard.

Where are the words with prefixes?

March I4, 2002

Dear Art Scholars,
Yesterday's trip to the art museum
was very enriching and inspiring!
I really enjoyed viewing the art and
sharing dialogue with you about it.
What ideas did you learn from our
visit that you might choose to incorporate into your own work?

Math Challenge: What is the fraction
that will tell how many rooms we
were able to visit yesterday out of the
total number of rooms at the Museum?

Sixth Grade

**Sample
Morning
Message
Charts**

September 28, 2001

Good Morning, Journalists,
During our writing period today we
need to complete all the preparation
for our interviews. We will talk about
these questions in meeting today. Bring
your thoughts.
What is an interview?
What is the purpose of our interviews?
How can we prepare for an interview?
Write an interesting, useful, and
appropriate interview question.

I'm eager to learn all about you!

Nov. 15, 2000

Dear Cooperative Students,
We will continue to work in our
history project groups today. I have
been impressed with each group's
creativity and productivity. I have also
noticed the positive ways that the
groups have been working together.
Share a strategy or a skill that you
think has helped your group.

How many synonyms can we come
up with for "cooperative"?

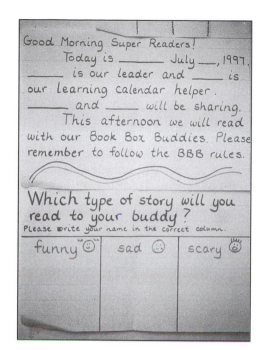

Appendix H

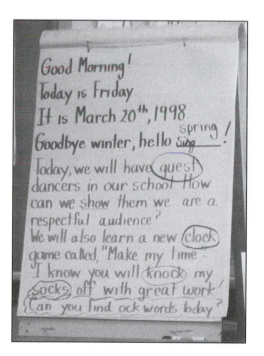

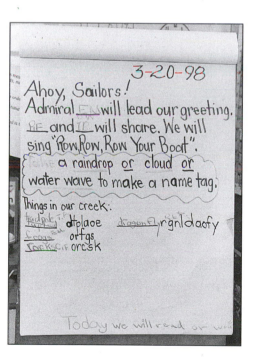

A sampling of Morning Message charts

REFERENCES

Berman, Sheldon. 1998. *Keynote Address at Responsive Leadership Institute, July 13.* Northeast Foundation for Children, Greenfield, MA.

Charney, Ruth S., Marlynn K. Clayton, Chip Wood. 1996. *Guidelines for The Responsive Classroom* (Training Manual). Greenfield, MA: Northeast Foundation for Children.

Crawford, Linda and Chip Wood. 1998. *Guidelines for The Responsive Classroom in Middle Schools* (Training Manual). Greenfield, MA: Northeast Foundation for Children.

Elias, Maurice J., Joseph E. Zins, Roger P. Weissberg, Karin S. Frey, Mark T. Greenberg, Norris M. Haynes, Rachael Kessler, Mary E. Schwab-Stone, Timothy P. Shriver. 1997. *Promoting Social and Emotional Learning: Guidelines for Educators.* Alexandria, VA: Association for Supervision and Curriculum Development.

Fraser, Jane and Donna Skolnick. 1994. *On Their Way: Celebrating Second Graders as They Read and Write.* Portsmouth, NH: Heinemann.

Goldsmith, Suzanne. Quoted in Glenda Valentine. 1998. "Don't Walk Away." *Teaching Tolerance* (Spring): 4.

Ilg, Francis L., MD, Louise Bates Ames, PhD, Sidney M. Baker, MD. 1981 (Revised Edition). *Child Behavior.* New York: Harper & Row.

Katz, Lilian. Interview by Karen Rasmussen. In "Early Childhood Education." Curriculum Update—*ASCD Newsletter* (Winter 1998): 1–8.

Lynn, Leon. 1997. "Language-Rich Home and School Environments Are Key to Reading Success." *The Harvard Education Letter* (July/August): 1–5.

Noddings, Nel. 1992. *The Challenge to Care in Schools: An Alternative Approach to Education.* New York: Teachers College Press.

Palmer, Parker J. 1998. *The Courage to Teach: Exploring the Inner Landscape of a Teacher's Life.* San Francisco: Jossey-Bass, Inc., Publishers.

Rogoff, Barbara. 1990. *Apprenticeship in Thinking: Cognitive Development in Social Context.* Oxford: Oxford University Press.

Sendak, Maurice. 1962. *Chicken Soup with Rice*. New York: HarperCollins.

Senge, Peter M., Charlotte Roberts, Richard B. Ross, Bryan J. Smith, and Art Kleiner. 1994. *The Fifth Discipline Fieldbook: Strategies and Tools for Building a Learning Organization*. New York: Currency Doubleday.

Wood, Chip. 1997. *Yardsticks, Children in the Classroom Ages 4–14. A Resource for Parents and Teachers*. Greenfield, MA: Northeast Foundation for Children.

ABOUT THE AUTHORS

Roxann Kriete is executive director of Northeast Foundation for Children (NEFC). She has worked at NEFC since 1985, first as a teacher, grades five through eight, and then as director of the publishing division. Before joining the NEFC staff, she taught high school English. She has a BA from Bucknell University.

Lynn Bechtel joined the writing and editorial staff at Northeast Foundation for Children in summer 2001 with many years experience as both a teacher and writer. Her BA is from University of Michigan. She also has an MAT and an MFA in writing, both from University of Massachusetts.

ABOUT THE
RESPONSIVE CLASSROOM® APPROACH

This book grew out of the work of Northeast Foundation for Children, Inc. (NEFC) and an approach to teaching known as the *Responsive Classroom* approach. Developed by classroom teachers, this approach consists of highly practical strategies for integrating social and academic learning throughout the school day.

Seven beliefs underlie this approach:

1. The social curriculum is as important as the academic curriculum.

2. How children learn is as important as what they learn: Process and content go hand in hand.

3. The greatest cognitive growth occurs through social interaction.

4. There is a specific set of social skills that children need to learn and practice in order to be successful academically and socially: cooperation, assertion, responsibility, empathy, and self-control.

5. Knowing the children we teach—individually, culturally, and developmentally—is as important as knowing the content we teach.

6. Knowing the families of the children we teach and encouraging their participation is as important as knowing the children we teach.

7. How we, the adults at school, work together to accomplish our shared mission is as important as our individual competence: Lasting change begins with the adult community.

More information and guidance on the *Responsive Classroom* approach are available through:

Publications and Resources

- Books, videos, and audios for elementary educators
- Website with an extensive library of free articles: www.responsiveclassroom.org
- Free quarterly newsletter for educators
- Professional development kits for school-based study
- The *Responsive* blog, with news, ideas, and advice from and for elementary educators

Professional Development Opportunities

- One-day and week-long workshops for teachers
- Coaching and consultations at individual schools and school districts
- Annual conference for school leaders

For details, contact:

RESPONSIVE CLASSROOM
NORTHEAST FOUNDATION FOR CHILDREN, INC.
85 Avenue A, Suite 204   P. O. Box 718
Turners Falls, MA 01376-0718
Phone 800-360-6332 or 413-863-8288
Fax 877-206-3952
www.responsiveclassroom.org

The Morning Meeting Book
By Roxann Kriete
with contributions by Lynn Bechtel

(2002) 228 pages ISBN 978-1-892989-09-3

Use Morning Meeting in your classroom to build community, increase students' investment in learning, and improve academic and social skills. This book features: ■ *Step-by-step guidelines for holding Morning Meeting* ■ *A chapter on Morning Meeting in middle schools* ■ *45 greetings and 66 group activities* ■ *Frequently asked questions and answers*

Sample Morning Meetings
in a *Responsive Classroom* (DVD and booklet)

(2009) 70 minutes ISBN 978-1-892989-30-7

See Morning Meetings in action: ■ *Four complete meetings in different classrooms—kindergarten, first grade, and third grade* ■ *Meetings in September, November, February, and April* ■ *Shows how you can adapt the meetings to fit your students' needs* ■ *28-page viewing guide focusing on classroom management strategies and teacher language*

Energizers!
88 Quick Movement Activities That Refresh and Refocus, K–6
By Susan Lattanzi Roser

(2009) 160 pages ISBN 978-1-892989-33-8

Give children two- to three-minute movement breaks throughout the day so they'll learn well. ■ *Chants, playful movements, short games, songs* ■ *Old favorites with new twists and original creations by the author* ■ *Can be used any time of the day, inside or outside* ■ *All energizers labeled by grade level and type*

The First Six Weeks of School
By Paula Denton and Roxann Kriete

(2000) 232 pages ISBN 978-1-892989-04-8

Structure the first weeks of school to lay the groundwork for a productive year of learning. ■ *Guidelines for the first six weeks, including daily plans for the first three weeks for grades K–2, grades 3–4, and grades 5–6* ■ *Ideas for building community, teaching routines, introducing engaging curriculum, fostering autonomy* ■ *Games, activities, greetings, songs, read-alouds, and resources especially useful during the early weeks of school*

Rules in School
By Kathryn Brady, Mary Beth Forton, Deborah Porter, and Chip Wood
(2003) 272 pages ISBN 978-1-892989-10-9

Establish a calm, safe learning environment and teach children self-discipline with this approach to classroom rules. ▪ *Guidelines for creating rules with students based on their hopes and dreams for school* ▪ *Steps in modeling and role-playing the rules* ▪ *How to reinforce the rules through language* ▪ *Using logical consequences when rules are broken* ▪ *Suggestions for teaching children to live by the rules outside the classroom*

The Power of Our Words:
Teacher Language that Helps Children Learn
By Paula Denton, EdD
(2007) 180 pages ISBN 978-1-892989-18-5

Use your words, tone, and speaking pace with intention to help students develop self-control, a sense of belonging, and academic skills. ▪ *The three Rs of teacher language: reinforcing, reminding, redirecting* ▪ *Open-ended questions that stretch children's thinking* ▪ *Listening and using silence skillfully*

Solving Thorny Behavior Problems:
How Teachers and Students Can Work Together
By Caltha Crowe
(2009) 304 pages ISBN 978-1-892989-32-1

Engage children in solving their own problems so they'll be invested, feel safe and challenged, and learn. ▪ *Problem-solving conferences* ▪ *Role-playing* ▪ *Conflict resolution* ▪ *Class meetings* ▪ *Individual written agreements*

Sammy and His Behavior Problems:
Stories and Strategies from a Teacher's Year
By Caltha Crowe
(2010) 168 pages ISBN 978-1-892989-31-4

Join third grade teacher Caltha Crowe as she works with Sammy, a student who had tantrums and meltdowns, scared other children, and defied teachers. ▪ *Rich stories complemented by the teacher's journal entries sharing her doubts, triumphs, and "Aha!" moments* ▪ *Accounts of real teacher-student interactions, from problem-solving conferences to respectful redirections* ▪ *Concrete strategies you can try with your own Sammy*

AVAILABLE FROM

www.responsiveclassroom.org ▪ 800-360-6332